Relish
SOUTH WEST
SECOND HELPING

Original recipes from the South West's
finest chefs and restaurants.
Introduction by chef Nathan Outlaw.

First Published 2016
By Relish Publications
Shield Green Farm, Tritlington,
Northumberland, NE61 3DX.

Twitter: @Relish_Cookbook
Facebook: RelishRestaurantGuide
For cookbooks and recipes visit:
www.relishpublications.co.uk
For publishing enquiries visit:
www.relish-publishing.co.uk

ISBN: 978-0-9934678-1-3

Publisher: Duncan L Peters
General Manager: Teresa Peters
Design: Vicki Brown
Publishing and Marketing Executive: Rebecca Laycock
Proofing Coordinator: Valerie McLeod
Sales: Wendy Rutterford
Relish Photography: Andy Richardson
www.awaywithmedia.com Twitter: @andyrichardson1
Editorial Consultant: Paul Robertson
Twitter: @paulrobbo1966

Front cover photograph by: Andy Richardson

Printed in Poland on behalf of Latitude Press

Welcome to this Second Helping of Relish South West; with a mouth-watering collection of recipes from the region's finest chefs and restaurants. We know you will enjoy cooking your way through the pages of this beautiful guide.

Since starting Relish Publications in 2009, we are privileged to have worked with hundreds of talented and highly acclaimed chefs, some of the biggest names in British food, and now have a national portfolio of over 25 regional fine-dining guides and bespoke recipe books.

There are more than 1500 signature dishes and restaurants for you to access on our website at www.relishpublications.co.uk. We have circumnavigated the UK in our hunt for the most highly acclaimed eateries, hidden gems and those highly recommended by other top chefs in the UK.

As the proud owner of a Relish cookbook you can also subscribe for a free Relish Rewards Card which entitles members to exclusive offers at some of the featured restaurants, ranging from a bottle of Champagne to free gifts when you dine.

We love to hear from our readers. If you have any questions about the recipes please email our friendly, qualified team - marketing@relishpublications.co.uk.

So, next time you're planning to dine in an outstanding restaurant or cook for friends, tantalise your tastebuds with one of our Relish recipe books, lie back and think of England, Scotland or Wales and enjoy planning your next meal!

Best wishes and bon appétit *Relish* x

004
CONTENTS

006
CONTENTS

Crab Pâté with Pink Grapefruit - **Page 100**

009
STARTERS

011
MAINS

013
DESSERTS

015

FOREWORD BY NATHAN OUTLAW

There was a time when if someone was asked about the food and drink in Cornwall and the South West, their mind immediately conjured visions of pasties, clotted cream and scrumpy cider. Nothing wrong with that! But we've come a long way since then and now I'm pleased to say that our area has become known as a gastronomic centre of excellence in the UK.

Having been brought up in Kent, I moved to Cornwall after working for a couple of years with top chefs in London. I knew Cornwall was going to become 'home' even when I visited on family holidays as a kid. From the moment I arrived as an 18-year-old commis chef to begin work with Rick Stein at The Seafood Restaurant in Padstow, it just felt right. The laid-back lifestyle suited me, the open spaces allowed me to breathe and never being far from the sea was a calming influence. And then there was the food...

Cornwall is unique in the UK in that we have a microclimate that means virtually anything grows here (even tea!). The mild winters mean that crops like new potatoes and asparagus are ready earlier than the rest of the country and the fact that we have copious amounts of rain also means we have lush pastures on which to graze our cattle. Oh, and being surrounded by the sea means we have access to the finest, freshest fish and seafood available in the country.

For a chef like me, Cornwall is a dream come true. I never tire of seeing what my producers bring me and each item of produce always inspires me to create a dish that truly does it justice. I've spent time building up fantastic relationships with my producers and know their passion equals mine, along with a desire to offer the very best they can to their customers.

And I'm not the only chef in Cornwall or the South West who feels this way. In recent years, others have taken their inspiration from our fantastic surroundings and now we can proudly boast a range of excellent restaurants where quality, locality and sustainability are coupled with ever-improving standards of cooking.

In this edition of Relish, you will find details of many of those restaurants and I'd recommend that if you value good food, you read up on what we have to offer, then take time out to visit Cornwall and the other areas in the South West to enjoy some of the wonderful food, drink and hospitality we have here. There's absolutely no doubt in my mind that in the South West the food and drink scene is fantastic!

Chef/Restaurateur Nathan Outlaw.

(Nathan's South West venues include Restaurant Nathan Outlaw, Port Isaac; Outlaw's Fish Kitchen, Port Isaac and The Mariners Public House, Rock.)

CHAPTER 1 RESTAURANT

8 Morfa Hall, Cliff Road, Newquay, Cornwall, TR7 1SG

01637 499 263
www.chapter1restaurant.co.uk Twitter: @ChefTomMackins

In early 2016, with help from family and friends, chef Tom Mackins risked everything to go it alone and he opened the doors of Chapter 1 Restaurant, at the age of only 25.

Located just off Cliff Road in the centre of Newquay, Chapter 1 is the perfect venue to relax and enjoy the best of Cornwall's culinary delights. "Chapter 1 was created with one thing in mind" says Tom, "unforgettable food with an affordable price tag."

The intimate, 24-cover, fine dining restaurant has an open kitchen, allowing guests to watch in awe and anticipation as Tom and his young team work hard to serve up flavoursome, fresh and locally sourced ingredients. In addition to the à la carte menu, which is accompanied by a very well selected and reasonably priced wine list, for the more adventurous diners there is also the option to sample some delicious culinary combinations on the extremely popular six-course tasting menu.

Tom started his career at an early age, travelling up and down the country working for some of the best restaurants and most respected hotels. In 2011 he moved to Cornwall to work for the well-respected Kevin Viner and, ever since, he has worked alongside some of the best chefs the South West has to offer.

"Opening a restaurant has been my dream for a very long time," says Tom. "Now that dream is a reality I'm already thinking about Chapter 2!"

"Chapter 1 was created with one thing in mind - unforgettable food with an affordable price tag." Chef Tom Mackins.

SQUID 'BLACK & WHITE'

SERVES 4

 *Riesling Viognier 2014
(Australia)*

Ingredients

Squid Ink Sponge

50ml vegetable oil
1 medium egg
50g caster sugar
1 sachet squid ink
150g self-raising flour
1 tsp baking powder

Cauliflower Purées

¼ onion (peeled, diced)
1 clove garlic (chopped)
1 head cauliflower
75g butter
full-fat milk (to cover)
1 sachet squid ink
1 tsp miso

Squid

12 baby squid tubes
100g cornflour
oil (for deep frying)

Method

For The Squid Ink Sponge (Prepare ahead)

Mix the vegetable oil, egg, sugar and sachet of squid ink together to a paste. Fold in the self-raising flour and baking powder. Microwave the mixture for 90 seconds. Remove the cake and break it into bite-size pieces. Place the cake into a dehydrator overnight until the cake is dry and crunchy.

For The Cauliflower Purées

Lightly fry the onion and garlic in a heavy-bottomed saucepan. Break the cauliflower into small florets and add to the pan (reserving 3 tiny florets for each person for later).
Add the butter to the pan and cover the mixture with milk. Cook for 15-20 minutes until the cauliflower is completely soft. Transfer to a jug blender and blend until smooth.

Remove half of the purée and set aside.

Add the squid ink and miso to the remaining purée in the blender and blend for 1 minute. Set aside.

For The Squid

Remove the squid tentacles and rinse under cold water for 2 minutes. Place the tentacles in a container with the cornflour.

Slice open the squid tubes and score the inside. Turn them over so the skin is facing upwards. Place on a metal tray and leave to come to room temperature.

To Serve

Warm up the cauliflower purées and splatter them onto your chosen plate.

Blanch the reserved cauliflower florets.

Deep fry (180°C) the squid tentacles for 30 seconds.

Blow torch the squid tubes until they have curled up and are just cooked.

Place the squid tubes onto the plate along with the cauliflower florets and squid tentacles. Finish with the dehydrated squid ink sponge.

Chef's Tip

Be creative and go crazy with the presentation of this dish.

RUN RABBIT RUN

SERVES 4

 *Domaine Durand Sancerre, Loire 2014
(France)*

Method

Ingredients

4 whole rabbits
8 slices Parma ham

Faggots And Spring Rolls

rabbit leg meat (from above)
50g dried apricots
2 tsp Dijon mustard
1 clove garlic
thyme (pinch of)
rabbit livers, hearts and kidneys (from above)
50g prunes
4 sheets spring roll pastry
1 egg (beaten with a dash of milk)
oil (for deep frying)

Red Wine Sauce

300ml red wine
1 litre chicken stock
1 litre veal stock
1 small bunch thyme
2 cloves garlic
3 black peppercorns
1 bay leaf

Carrot Purée

3 orange carrots (peeled, diced)
orange juice (to cover)
25g butter
salt and pepper

Baby And Purple Carrots

2 purple carrots
2 banana shallots
oil (drizzle of)
thyme (pinch of)
4 baby rainbow carrots

To Serve

1 kohlrabi (shaved with a potato peeler)
pistachio sponge (optional)

To Prepare The Rabbits
Remove the liver, heart and kidneys from the rabbits and set aside. Remove the legs and set aside. Bone out the loins and set aside.

For The Faggots And Spring Rolls
Blend the rabbit leg meat to a paste in a food processor with the apricots, mustard, garlic and thyme. Remove half of the paste and set aside.
Add the liver, heart and kidneys to the food processor and continue to blend with half of the paste until smooth. Roll into small balls to make the faggots. Set aside.
Divide the reserved paste into 4 and roll into small logs. Lay out the sheets of pastry and spread the paste on. Carefully roll up the pastry ensuring that the paste is fully enclosed. Egg wash to secure, then set aside.

For The Red Wine Sauce
Reduce the red wine to a sticky glaze in a saucepan. Add the remaining ingredients and continue to reduce to 300ml. Strain and keep warm.

For The Rabbit Loins
Remove any sinew and wrap 2 loins together with 2 slices of Parma ham. Roll the loins in cling film and tie them at both ends ready to poach. Place the wrapped loins into a pan of simmering water and cook for 8 minutes. Remove from the water, unwrap and leave to rest.

Chef's Tip
Be careful not to overcook the rabbit.

For The Carrot Purée
Place the carrots into a heavy-bottomed pan and cover with orange juice. Cook for 30 minutes or until soft. Blend with the butter. Season to taste.

For The Baby And Purple Carrots
Preheat the oven to 210°C.
Place the purple carrots and shallots on an oven tray. Drizzle with oil and sprinkle with thyme. Cover with tin foil and roast in the oven for 30 minutes, then cut the carrots in half. Boil the baby carrots for 5 minutes.

To Serve
Place the faggots into a small pan with the red wine sauce and cook for 6 minutes. Add the prunes and cook for a further 2 minutes.
Deep fry (180°C) the spring rolls for 3 minutes or until golden. Smear the carrot purée across the plate. Cut the loins and spring rolls in half and place onto the purée. Plate the roasted carrots, shallots and baby carrots. Add the shaved kohlrabi to the plate. Finish with the faggots and drizzle over the sauce.

THE 'GOLD BAR'

SERVES 4

 *Villa Maria Sauvignon Blanc 2014
(New Zealand)*

Ingredients

Chocolate Casing

50g white chocolate

Chocolate Mousse

100g white chocolate
220ml double cream
3 egg whites

Caramel

250g caster sugar
90g butter (diced)
125ml double cream
1 tsp salt

To Serve

edible gold spray
ice cream or sorbet (optional)
ginger biscuit crumb

4 bar-shaped silicone moulds

Method

For The Chocolate Casing

Carefully melt the white chocolate in a microwave until completely smooth. Brush the melted chocolate into the silicone moulds and freeze.

For The Chocolate Mousse

Melt the chocolate and leave to cool down.

Whip the cream to soft peaks, then whip the egg whites to stiff peaks.

Once the chocolate has cooled, fold it in to the cream. Carefully fold in the egg whites and place into a piping bag. Store in the fridge until needed.

For The Caramel

Melt the sugar to a golden caramel in a heavy-bottomed pan. Gradually stir the butter into the hot sugar. Once combined, slowly add the cream and simmer for 5 minutes. Whisk in the salt and remove from the heat. Leave to cool.

Place the cooled caramel into the white chocolate shell until half filled. Pipe on the mousse and place in the freezer for 2 hours.

To Serve

Pop the bars out from the shells and spray with edible gold spray. Serve immediately with the ginger biscuit crumb topped with your choice of ice cream or sorbet; ginger and lime sorbet works well.

Chef's Tip

Keep it simple.

CONSTANTINE RESTAURANT

AT TREVOSE GOLF & COUNTRY CLUB

Constantine Bay, Padstow, Cornwall, PL28 8JB

01841 520 208
www.trevose-gc.co.uk Twitter: Constantine@Trevose

Located on the edge of the North Cornwall coastline is Trevose Golf and Country Club, home to Constantine Restaurant, which is blessed with some of the most spectacular views in the UK.

From the bar and restaurant's panoramic windows, the view stretches out towards Trevose Head and the Atlantic Ocean; over sand dunes, streams and the tamarisk dotted fairways to Booby's Bay, Mackerel Cove and, far out at sea, the Quies Rocks.

Head chef Dan Clark and his team work hard to create a menu befitting such a location.

Constantine Restaurant aims to offer guests a little piece of gourmet heaven on the north Cornish coast, delivering quality local seafood, meat and fresh produce straight to the plate.

Having spent his time learning the trade in some of the finest establishments in the UK - formerly at the Kensington Hotel in London - Dan now prides himself on sourcing and using the best ingredients from local suppliers in the South West of England.

As well as offering delicious food, the club boasts many facilities, including the amazing 18-hole championship golf course, which diners can overlook and admire in all its glory.

Owned by the Gammon family since 1955, personal family values remain fundamental to Trevose's unique charm and character, providing guests with a friendly, welcoming and relaxing atmosphere.

"Pushing the restaurant forward and developing the team, inspiring the next generation of chefs, sourcing local fresh produce to offer guests the best possible dishes - that is the focus."
Dan Clark, head chef.

WHIPPED GOAT'S CHEESE WITH BEETROOT & HERB SALAD

SERVES 4

 Sables d'Azur 2014, Côtes de Provence (France)

Ingredients

Whipped Goat's Cheese

200g soft goat's cheese
75g cream cheese
1 tbsp olive oil
salt (pinch of)

Beetroot And Herb Salad

1 raw, striped beetroot (peeled)
2 cooked beetroots (mixed colours)
olive oil (drizzle of)
seasoning

Walnut Dressing

1 tbsp walnut oil
3 tbsp white wine vinegar
1 tbsp runny honey
seasoning

Garnish

40g soft British herbs (chervil, dill, chives, mint, parsley)

2-3cm round, non-fluted cutter

Method

For The Whipped Goat's Cheese

Add the goat's cheese, cream cheese, olive oil and a pinch of salt to a bowl and whisk until blended and smooth. Place into a piping bag and leave to rest at room temperature until required.

For The Beetroot

Slice the raw beetroot as thinly as possible. Using a small, round, non-fluted cutter, cut into rounds and toss with seasoned olive oil.

Cut the cooked beetroots into a mixture of 1cm dice and matchsticks, ensuring you have both shapes in both colours.

Chef's Tip

Use an independent greengrocer who is likely to have more varieties of beetroot.

For The Walnut Dressing

Whisk the walnut oil, vinegar and honey with a little seasoning.

To Serve

Arrange the raw and cooked beetroot randomly around the plate. Pipe the goat's cheese into 7 or 8 small towers to create height. Place the picked herbs across the plate, drizzle with the walnut dressing and serve immediately.

CORNISH HAKE FILLET, MUSSELS, PARSLEY SAUCE

SERVES 4

 Mâcon-Lugny
(France)

Ingredients

Vegetables

400g Cornish new potatoes
20g butter
2 shallots (diced)
olive oil (drizzle of)
salt and pepper (to season)
1 courgette (sliced)
2 tomatoes

Parsley Sauce

900ml fish stock
450ml double cream
100g parsley (chopped)

Hake And Mussels

butter (knob of)
4 x 160g hake fillets (seasoned)
320g mussels (steamed prior to serving)

Garnish

140g samphire (steamed)

Method

For The Vegetables

Cover the potatoes in water and bring to the boil. Cook until soft, then remove from the heat and add the butter.

Gently fry the shallots without colouring in a little oil until soft. Add to the potatoes, then crush with a fork. Check the seasoning.

Slice the courgette into 12 equal slices. Cook in boiling, salted water for several minutes.

Score the tomatoes and place in boiling, salted water for 2 minutes until the skin starts to come off. Plunge into ice cold water and once cooled, use a knife to remove the skin. Cut into quarters and remove the seeds. Cut the flesh into 2cm dice.

For The Parsley Sauce

Pour the fish stock into a pan, bring to the boil and reduce by half. Add the cream and simmer for 5 minutes. Remove from the heat and keep warm.

For The Hake Fillet And Mussels

Heat a large pan with a knob of butter. Place the seasoned hake skin-side down into the pan and cook for 4-5 minutes. Turn over and cook for a further 2-3 minutes.

Add the mussels to a pan with a small amount of the sauce, place the lid on top and steam until they are fully opened, discarding any that do not open.

Chef's Tip

Buy the freshest fish you can and ask your fishmonger to prepare the fish for you. This will save you time in the kitchen.

To Plate

Using a ring mould for neat presentation if desired, place the crushed potatoes in the centre of the plate. Lay the courgette slices on top of the potatoes and top with the hake, skin-side up.

Scatter the tomatoes and samphire and arrange the mussels around the plate. To finish, add the parsley to the warm sauce and pour over the dish.

STRAWBERRY JELLY WITH ELDERFLOWER CREAM & SORBET

SERVES 6

Château Petit Védrines 2011, Sauternes (France)

Ingredients

Strawberry Jelly

500g strawberries (reserve a few to go inside the jelly)
150g granulated sugar
300ml water
2 leaves gelatine (soaked in cold water)

Elderflower Cream

100ml double cream
40ml elderflower cordial

Elderflower Sorbet

200g caster sugar
500ml water
250ml elderflower cordial

To Garnish

seasonal edible flowers

6 serving glasses

Method

For The Strawberry Jelly (Prepare ahead)

Cut the strawberries in half and add to a pan with the sugar and water. Bring to the boil and simmer for a few minutes.

Remove from the heat and pass through a fine sieve. Cool in the fridge for 25-35 minutes.

Divide the mixture in 2, placing half in a pan. Gently reheat the pan and, as the liquid warms, stir in the gelatine leaves to dissolve them. Once fully dissolved, pour the contents of the pan back into the cooled liquid.

Place the reserved strawberries into the glasses. Pour the strawberry jelly over and place in the fridge until set, about 3-4 hours.

For The Elderflower Cream

Gently whisk the cream and elderflower cordial in a bowl until it forms soft peaks. Transfer to a piping bag and pipe the mixture on top of the set jelly.

For The Elderflower Sorbet (Prepare ahead)

Bring the sugar and water to the boil in a saucepan. Keep stirring until the sugar dissolves. Remove from the heat and stir in the elderflower cordial.

Place in a large bowl and chill in the fridge for about 4 hours, or overnight if possible.

Churn in an ice cream machine, then pour into a container and place in the freezer. Stir every hour until frozen.
(This will take approximately 6-7 hours depending on your freezer temperature).

Chef's Tip

If you're pushed for time or do not own an ice cream machine, cheat and use a shop bought elderflower sorbet. It is now really popular and widely available.

To Serve

Remove the sorbet from the freezer just before serving to soften slightly. Place the elderflower sorbet on top of the elderflower cream and garnish with the seasonal edible flowers.

036
THE HARBOUR RESTAURANT

The Metropole Hotel, Station Road, Padstow, Cornwall, PL28 8DB

01841 532 486
www.the-metropole.co.uk Twitter: @The_Metropole

Situated high above the small fishing town of Padstow, the AA Rosette award-winning Harbour Restaurant is on the perfect vantage point to appreciate the beauty of one of Cornwall's most famous towns. The contemporary, yet elegantly designed restaurant, feels perfectly at home in the grandeur of the Victorian built 4 star Metropole Hotel with its high ceilings and large and plentiful traditional sash windows. The Harbour Restaurant is the perfect place to take in unrivalled views of the ever changing Camel Estuary and pretty, stone built, Cornish town.

Head chef Mike Corbin has a passion for great flavours and letting local, quality ingredients do the talking. In a town renowned for its seafood, the team at The Harbour Restaurant pride themselves on delivering, clean-tasting, locally inspired flavours, consistently presented with the precision and flair you would expect from a team with a young and dynamic edge.

Mike and his team's creative and honest approach to food, accompanied by an extensive collection of expertly selected wines, the perfect Cornish location, exceptional setting and outstanding service is what consistently gives their customers a truly unforgettable fine dining experience.

With views across the Estuary and Padstow Harbour, you can dine in the AA Rosette Harbour Restaurant or the more casual Brasserie @ The Met where the food is fresh, seasonal and a true taste of the South West.

CORNISH CRAB WITH AVOCADO PUREE & CHILLI OIL

SERVES 4

*Domaine Serge Laporte, Loire 2014
(France)*

Cornish Crab

200g handpicked white crab meat
15g crème fraîche
15g mayonnaise
½ lemon (juice of)
10g coriander (chopped)
5g chives (chopped)
salt (to taste)

Avocado Purée

2 ripe avocados (peeled, de-stoned)
1 lime (juice of)
30g coriander leaf
½ chilli
salt (to taste)
30ml olive oil

Chilli Oil

100ml olive oil
20g red chilli (finely sliced)

Garnish

8 pink grapefruit segments
1 radish (thinly sliced)
¼ red chilli (finely chopped)

Method

For The Cornish Crab

Check the crab meat to ensure there is no shell. Combine all the ingredients with the crab meat. Keep in the fridge until ready to serve.

For The Avocado Purée

Blend all the ingredients in a blender, then pass through a fine sieve. Store in an airtight piping bag in the fridge until required.

For The Chilli Oil (Prepare ahead)

Gently warm the oil in a pan, add the chilli and leave to infuse. Cool to room temperature.

To Serve

Quenelle the crab mix onto the plate and place 2 pink grapefruit segments to one side. Pipe a small amount of the avocado purée next to the crab and sprinkle the top with a few thin slices of radish and fresh chilli. Drizzle with a little chilli oil.

Chef's Tip

When making *quenelles* out of cold foods like ice cream, it's sometimes helpful to run a little hot water over the spoon to heat it before scooping. Try lots of different spoons to see which you like best for the job.

PORK FOUR WAYS

SERVES 4

Agostino Petri da Vicchiomaggio, Chianti Classico DOCG Tuscany 2011 (Italy)

Ingredients

Pig Cheeks

olive oil (to fry), 4 pig cheeks (trimmed)
100ml Cornish cider, 50ml chicken stock
2½g paprika 5g fennel seeds
1g salt, 50g butter (diced)

Pork Fillet

1 pork fillet (trimmed, cut in half)
5g Dijon mustard, 2½g fennel seeds
5g tarragon, 1g salt

Pork Belly

600g pork belly
250ml apple juice, 250ml chicken stock
5g tarragon, 1g salt

Black Pudding Bon Bon

100g black pudding, 5g tarragon
5g plain flour (seasoned)
5g Japanese panko
1 large free-range egg (beaten)

Cauliflower Purée

¼ cauliflower (diced), 15g butter
35ml full-fat milk, 35ml double cream

Roasted Cauliflower and Crispy Cauliflower Leaf

¼ cauliflower (florets of)
5g butter, 1 cauliflower leaf
oil (for deep frying), salt

Toasted Hazelnuts

50g hazelnuts, 1 tsp olive oil

Cauliflower Potato Mash

50g cauliflower purée (see above)
250g Maris Piper potato mash
salt and pepper (to season)

Sauce

2 tbsp tarragon (coarsely chopped)
1 lemon (zest and juice of)
2 large cloves garlic (minced)
2 tbsp Dijon mustard
½ cup extra virgin olive oil
50ml cider

Method

For The Pig Cheeks

Preheat the oven to 130°C (fan).

Heat a large ovenproof dish on the hob. Once hot, add the olive oil and fry the cheeks in batches until they are golden brown. Set aside. Add the cider to the pan and cook gently for 3-4 minutes. Return the cheeks to the dish.

Increase the heat and cook until the liquid has reduced by half, then add the chicken stock, paprika, fennel seeds and salt. Cover and transfer the dish to the oven and cook for 2-2½ hours until tender.

Strain the liquid into a separate pot. Reduce the sauce by half, then gradually add the butter until you have a thick sauce. Put the cheeks in the sauce and warm through.

For The Pork Fillet

Combine all the ingredients and marinate the pork for 2 hours. Preheat the oven to 200°C (fan).

Brown the pork in a little oil, transfer to the oven and roast for 15-20 minutes until the meat reaches 63°C on a thermometer.

For The Pork Belly

Preheat the oven to 180°C (fan).

Combine all the ingredients. Lay the pork skin-side up and bake for 2¼ hours. Increase the oven temperature to 200°C for a further 35 minutes to crisp the crackling. Rest for 10-15 minutes before carving.

For The Black Pudding Bon Bon

Blitz the pudding and tarragon together and shape into 4 small balls. *Pane,* then deep fry (170°C) until golden.

For The Cauliflower Purée

Simmer the cauliflower until tender. Strain, blend with the remaining ingredients, then pass through a fine sieve.

For The Roasted Cauliflower And Crispy Cauliflower Leaf

Boil the florets until tender. Air dry, then roast in a pan in butter until golden. Briefly deep fry the leaf (170°C) until crisp. Rest on kitchen paper. Sprinkle with salt.

For The Toasted Hazelnuts

Toast the hazelnuts in a pan with a little oil until golden brown. Allow to cool and remove the skins. Break up into small pieces.

For The Cauliflower Potato Mash

Stir the purée into the mash, season well. Place in a piping bag.

For The Sauce

Reduce the braising juices from the cheeks with the sauce ingredients until thick.

To Serve

Serve as pictured.

BUTTERMILK PANNA COTTA, MARINATED STRAWBERRIES, PISTACHIO SPONGE, STRAWBERRY SORBET

SERVES 4

Max Ferd Richter Mülheimer Helenenkloster, Riesling Eiswein, Mosel Prädikatswein, 2012 (Germany)

Ingredients

Buttermilk Panna Cotta

50g sugar
20ml boiled water
2 leaves gelatine (soaked in cold water)
1 vanilla pod (seeds of)
250ml double cream
125ml buttermilk

Strawberry Sorbet

250ml strawberry purée
250ml sugar syrup

Marinated Strawberries

75ml strawberry purée
75ml stock syrup
elderflower cordial (dash of)
¼ vanilla pod
100g strawberries (hulled)

Pistachio Sponge

75g pistachios (peeled)
75g sugar
20g self-raising flour
4 egg whites

4 dariole moulds (7½cm x 5cm)

Method

For The Buttermilk Panna Cotta (Prepare ahead)

Bring the sugar and water up to 118°C. Stir in the softened gelatine and leave to rest for 1 minute. Add in the vanilla seeds, cream and buttermilk. Pour into the moulds and set in the fridge for 4 hours, or overnight.

Chef's Tip

Panna cotta is such a simple dish that both the flavour and the texture must be 'just so' - there really is nowhere to hide. Once you've mastered the recipe, it's the perfect make-ahead stuff for those occasions when Angel Delight just won't do!

For The Strawberry Sorbet

Mix the ingredients together, churn in an ice cream machine and freeze.

For The Marinated Strawberries

Warm up the strawberry purée, stock syrup, cordial and vanilla. Add the fresh strawberries and leave the mix to cool and infuse. If you have a vac pac machine, you can compress this to intensify the flavour.

For The Pistachio Sponge

Blend all ingredients until bright green in colour. Pass through a fine sieve. Place 4 spoonfuls of the mixture onto greaseproof paper and cook in the microwave for 40 seconds until light and fluffy.

To Serve

Turn the panna cotta out of the mould onto a plate. Add a scoop of the strawberry sorbet. Dot the marinated strawberries and arrange pieces of the pistachio sponge around the plate.

046
IDLE ROCKS HOTEL

Tredenham Road, St Mawes, Cornwall, TR2 5AN

01326 270 270
www.idlerocks.com Twitter: @TheIdleRocks

The Idle Rocks is a top British luxury retreat owned by David and Karen Richards; the 19-bedroom boutique hotel has a destination restaurant run by head chef Guy Owen.

Guy joined the team in July 2015 and has introduced a menu championing Cornish food - working with local fishermen, greengrocers and sourcing the best meat from the West Country. By taking advantage of the local waters, Guy showcases not only the fish and shellfish available on the doorstep but also sea vegetables in abundance from the coastline, such as seaweed, samphire and sea pea.

The Hampshire born chef developed his culinary expertise with some of London's leading chefs, including Gordon Ramsay in his Michelin starred restaurant at Claridges, Jerome Tauvron at L'Etranger and James Bennington and Bruce Poole at Michelin starred La Trompette. More recently, since returning to the West Country in 2009, Guy worked at leading hotels including Gidleigh Park, under the direction of Michael Caines, and the Driftwood Hotel, where he became sous chef under Chris Eden.

Guy's passion for food is fuelled by the wonderful Cornish produce and the menu at The Idle Rocks reflects the hotel's ethos of re-engaging with the simple pleasures in life. Guests can relax in a simply stunning setting - the restaurant and terrace both south-facing, overlooking wonderful sea views.

There is a relaxed but lively atmosphere, with music playing, guests chattering, cocktails being created and a great wine list to mull over and enjoy.

Idyllically situated on the Harbourside of St Mawes and recently awarded membership of Relais and Châteaux, Idle Rocks is home from home where you can make yourself comfortable and re-engage with the simpler pleasures in life.

CHARRED MACKEREL, VEGETABLES A LA GRECQUE

SERVES 4

 Turning Heads Sauvignon Blanc, Marlborough (New Zealand)

Ingredients

Liquor
80ml olive oil
80ml white wine vinegar
160ml water
160ml dry white wine
3 sprigs thyme
1 clove garlic (crushed)
20 fennel seeds
15 coriander seeds
8 black peppercorns
2 bay leaves

Vegetables à La Grecque
2 medium heritage carrots (peeled)
1 sprig thyme
Cornish sea salt (to season)
8 baby carrots (peeled)
4 baby courgette
2 banana shallots (peeled)

Brown Crab Mayonnaise
200g homemade or shop bought mayonnaise
100g brown crab meat
salt (to season)
lemon juice (to taste)

Chervil Purée
1 bunch chervil
baby leaf spinach (handful of)
salt (pinch of)

Mackerel
2 large Cornish mackerel (filleted, v-cut)
olive oil
salt

Garnish
borage leaves
edible flowers

Method

For The Liquor
Combine all ingredients together and heat up in a pan to 80°C. Leave to infuse until cold.

For The Vegetables à La Grecque
Preheat the oven to 180°C (fan).
Wrap the heritage carrots in tin foil with some Cornish sea salt and a sprig of thyme. Bake in the oven for about 30 minutes until tender (test this with the tip of a knife). When cool enough to handle, cut into small batons.
Cut 4 of the baby carrots lengthways using a potato peeler to form ribbons. Repeat with the baby courgettes and set aside.
Cut across the shallots to form thin, mini onion rings. Keep the larger rings, discarding the tiny middles.
Strain the liquor through a fine sieve and divide between 4 small pans. Add the courgettes, carrot ribbons and shallots into separate pans, bring to 80°C, then remove from the heat and leave to cool. Add the whole carrots to the remaining pan and cook until tender.

For The Brown Crab Mayonnaise
Blend together the brown crab meat and mayonnaise in a liquidiser until smooth. Season with salt and lemon juice to taste.

For The Chervil Purée
Place the chervil in boiling water and cook for 2 minutes. Add the spinach and continue to cook for a further 3 minutes. Remove from the water and chill rapidly in ice water. Once cooled, remove from the water and place into a liquidiser. Add a little water and salt, then blend to a smooth, vibrant, green purée. Transfer to a bowl over ice water and cool rapidly.

For The Mackerel
Set the grill on a high heat.
Rub a little olive oil onto the mackerel skin and season with salt. Lay the mackerel flesh-side down on a tray and place directly under the grill, about 5-7cm away from the element, and cook. The mackerel skin will start to blister and char. Once the mackerel has cooked, if it hasn't blistered enough, finish off using a blow torch to give it a lovely smoky flavour.

To Assemble
Place 3 of the salt baked carrot batons to the side of the plate to form a semi-circle. Delicately follow the arc with the carrot ribbons and courgette ribbons, curling them to give height. Add a few shallot rings. Dot the plate with crab mayonnaise and chervil purée. Cut the whole baby carrots in half and lay these and the mackerel on the plate. Garnish with the borage leaves and edible flowers.

WILD BLACK BREAM ALLA ROMANA

SERVES 4

 Whispering Angel Provence Rosé
(France)

Ingredients

4 wild Cornish black bream (scaled, filleted, deboned)

Romana Sauce

200g unsalted butter (melted)
30g superfine capers
30g brown anchovies
3 cloves garlic (peeled)
flat leaf parsley (handful of, picked)
5 stems tarragon leaves (picked)
8 pitted green olives
salt (pinch of)
lemon juice (squeeze of)

Smoked Aubergine Purée

2 aubergines (blow torched, skins burnt)
2 sprigs thyme
salt (pinch of)
olive oil (drizzle of)
2 banana shallots
1 clove garlic
40ml double cream
40g passata
salt (pinch of)
lemon (squeeze of)

Red Pepper Purée

2 banana shallots (peeled, thinly sliced)
4 red peppers (skinned, cut into small pieces)
olive oil
20g butter
1 clove garlic

Barbecued Vegetables

2 courgettes (quartered, seeds removed)
2 red peppers (peeled, cut into quarters)
1 aubergine (cut into 8 long pieces)
12 new potatoes (cooked)
4 spring onions
4 green chillies

Method

For The Romana Sauce

Place all the ingredients in a liquidiser and blend until smooth. Season with salt and lemon juice.

For The Smoked Aubergine Purée

Preheat the oven to 180°C (fan).

Wrap the charred aubergines in tin foil with a little thyme, salt and olive oil. Bake in the oven for 10-15 minutes until completely soft. Remove the foil and place into a liquidiser with the remaining ingredients. Blend until smooth. Season with lemon juice and salt.

For The Red Pepper Purée

Sweat the banana shallots until tender, add the red peppers and continue to cook until soft. Add the remaining ingredients and continue to cook for a further 20 minutes on a low heat. Transfer to a liquidiser and blend until smooth.

For The Barbecued Vegetables

Barbecue the vegetables until soft to give nice griddle marks and a lovely flavour. Transfer to a tray and drizzle with a little of the Romana sauce. Toss, season and leave to cool naturally.

To Cook The Cornish Black Bream

Rub the black bream with a little olive oil and salt. Cook skin-side down on the barbecue until coloured. If they need to be cooked a little longer, transfer to the oven to finish at 180°C (fan) for 5 minutes.

Chef's Tip

Be sure to use the freshest and best quality black bream that you can get your hands on. I recommend the wonderful wild Cornish black bream from our fabulous supplier Wing of St Mawes.

To Assemble

Place a good sized portion of aubergine purée on the plate and run a spoon through it to create a 'tick', then splash a little of the red pepper purée on the plate. Arrange the barbecued vegetables neatly, so they are all in view. Rest the cooked black bream up against the vegetables and finish with a generous covering of the Romana sauce.

KAFFIR LIME SORBET, CUCUMBER, MINT & LIMONCELLO

SERVES 6

Knightor Non-Vintage Brut, Cornwall (England)

Method

For The Kaffir Lime Sorbet

Combine all the ingredients, except the lime leaves, in a pan and heat until the sugar has dissolved. Once dissolved, infuse with the kaffir lime leaves for 10 minutes and leave to cool. Place in a 'paco jet' container or churn in an ice cream machine. Freeze until required.

For The Cucumber And Mint

Cook half of the mint leaves in boiling water and, once cooked, cool rapidly in ice water. Place the cooked mint, fresh mint and sugar stock syrup into a blender and blend until smooth. Combine with the diced cucumber, then smell it - it is one of the best smells in the universe, in my opinion!

Chef's Tip

To tell if the mint is cooked, remove a leaf from the boiling water and rub between your index finger and thumb firmly; if the leaf breaks apart it is ready, if it rolls up into a leathery ball, it isn't.

To Assemble And Serve

Place some digestive biscuit crumble in the centre of a bowl. Scatter the minted cucumber over the crumble and around the bowl. Place a scoop of sorbet on top of the crumble, then add the crystallised honey (which you can warm up and shape any way you wish).

Pour a small shot (I say small, but those who love the stuff go bigger if you wish) of limoncello. Serve with the shot next to the dish and have your guests pour their shots over the sorbet and dessert. Enjoy - a totally fresh and fantastic way to finish a meal.

Ingredients

Kaffir Lime Sorbet

200g sugar
100g glucose
500ml water
170ml lime juice
5g ProSorbet
2 limes (zest of)
8 kaffir lime leaves (chopped)

Cucumber And Mint

1 bunch mint (leaves picked)
1 cucumber (seeds removed, finely diced)
300ml sugar stock syrup
salt (pinch of)

To Serve

digestive biscuits (crumbled)
6 limoncello shots
crystallised honey (purchased from specialist suppliers, could be replaced with bee pollen)
fresh mint leaves

056
KOTA RESTAURANT WITH ROOMS

Harbour Head, Porthleven, Cornwall, TR13 9JA

01326 562 407
www.kotarestaurant.co.uk Twitter: @JudeKereama

The translation is simple - Kota is Maori for shellfish. The name of the restaurant reflects both the gastronomic philosophy and cultural heritage of head chef Jude Kereama.

A star of BBC TV's Great British Menu and the holder of a Michelin Bib Gourmand, Jude, and his wife Jane, moved to Porthleven in Cornwall in 2004. Seduced by outstanding produce and exquisite harbourside views, they have developed their destination restaurant during more than a decade of hard graft.

Buying the finest shellfish from day boat fishermen, the freshest greens from seaside foragers and exceptional produce from further inland, they satisfy the culinary daydreams of discerning diners from across the South West.

An added bonus at Kota are the two bed and breakfast rooms, one with stunning harbour views, so customers can completely relax with a bottle of fine wine, a great night's sleep and finish off with Jude's fabulous breakfast.

More recently, Jude and Jane took on a separate restaurant, converting a former second-hand furniture warehouse into a light and airy bistro.

As the sun streams in through large plate glass windows, they serve huge crowds during spring, summer and autumn.

"There was very little here when we arrived," says Jude. "But we've worked hard and Porthleven is now a genuine foodie destination. There are lots of great restaurants including our two - even Rick Stein has moved in. It's very much on the map."

Jude grew up in New Zealand. His mother is Chinese/Malay and his father Maori. Those disparate influences are reflected in his clean and invigorating food. Flavours from China, Japan and beyond are paired with award-winning produce from the South West, creating an exotically pan-global cuisine that is both innovative and refreshing. "Even the fish and chips has a wasabi tartare," laughs Jane.

Jude and Jane, together with their dedicated team of staff, work tirelessly to create the finest food and service in a relaxed environment, achieving a Michelin Bib Gourmand, 2 AA Rosettes, and a score of 4 in the Good Food guide.

SEARED FALMOUTH BAY SCALLOPS, FIVE-SPICE BELLY OF PORK, CARROT STAR ANISE PUREE, APPLE GINGER DRESSING

SERVES 4

 Jim Barry 'Lodge Hill' Riesling, Clare Valley (Australia)

Ingredients

12 king scallops (prepared, patted dry)

Pork Belly

1 kg pork belly
2 tsp five-spice powder
100g Cornish sea salt
400ml boiling water
1 onion (sliced)
2 stalks celery (sliced)
1 thumb ginger (peeled, sliced)

Carrot Star Anise Purée

2 carrots (peeled, finely sliced)
2 carrots (juiced)
250ml cold water
1 star anise
150ml double cream

Apple Ginger Dressing

75ml rice vinegar
200ml Kikkoman soy sauce
50ml mirin
1 Granny Smith apple (skin on, finely grated)
½ thumb ginger root (finely grated)
1 clove garlic (finely grated)
75g white onion (finely grated)
50ml apple juice

Carrots

6 baby carrots (peeled)
butter (knob of)
Cornish sea salt (pinch of)

Garnish

1 pink radish (finely sliced)
coriander micro cress
pea shoots

Method

For The Pork Belly (Prepare ahead)

Score the skin of the pork belly and rub the five-spice and sea salt mix into the belly. Refrigerate overnight.

Preheat the oven to 150°C (fan).

Wipe any excess marinade off the pork belly. Place the onions, celery, ginger and boiling water in the bottom of a roasting tray and place the pork belly on top. Cover with a tight fitting lid or tin foil. Bake in the oven for 2½ hours until just tender. Cool, then place between 2 trays with a weight on top. Chill until set. Cut 12 slices and chop the rest into nice blocks for roasting another time.

For The Carrot Star Anise Purée

Place everything in a pot, except for the cream, and cook until the carrots are tender, topping up with water if needed. Reduce to a syrup, then add the cream. Bring to the boil and reduce by half. Remove the star anise and blend until very smooth. Season with salt and pepper, then pass through a fine sieve. Keep warm in a squeezy bottle until needed.

For The Apple Ginger Dressing

Add all the ingredients together and leave to infuse.

For The Carrots

Place the carrots in a vac pac bag with a knob of butter and a pinch of Cornish sea salt. Cook in a water bath on 80°C for 40 minutes until cooked. Refresh in an ice bath. Cut in half and keep for pan frying.

To Serve

Brown the pork belly and caramelise the baby carrots in a warm frying pan. Reserve in a warm area.

Bring another pan up to a medium heat, add the scallops, season and caramelise on one side. Turn and caramelise on the other side and add a knob of butter. Baste the scallops with the foaming butter until just cooked. Rest in a warm place.

Squeeze the carrot purée into 3 circles on the plate and put 3 pieces of pork belly on top of each purée circle. Place 3 scallops and 3 baby carrot halves on each plate. Dress with apple ginger dressing and garnish with radish discs, coriander cress and pea shoots.

Chef's Tip

Make sure to not overcook the scallops as they will become rubbery. When in season, it's good to add broad beans, asparagus or edamame beans.

NORI WRAPPED CORNISH HAKE WITH MUSSELS, COCKLES, SEAWEED, CRISPY ROCK SHRIMP, CRAB RAVIOLO, DASHI

SERVES 4

 Muscadet 'Le Pallet', Loire (France)

Ingredients

Dashi Stock

10cm square kombu, 2 litres spring water
75g bonito flakes, 100ml sake
100ml Japanese white soy sauce (shoyu)
2 yuzu fruit (juice of)

Squid Ink Pasta Dough

1 large, free range egg
14g squid ink, ½ tsp salt
125g pasta flour

Crab Ravioli Filling

75g lemon sole fillet
½ tsp salt
150ml double cream
white pepper (pinch of)
50g white crab meat (picked)
25g brown crab meat

Hake

4 hake fillets (8cm x 4cm approximately)
4 sheets nori

Shellfish

20 mussels (washed, beards removed)
20 cockles (purged in water)

Garnish

1 tin wasabi caviar
50g dried Cornish seagreens
50g dried Cornish red dulse seaweed
50g dried wakame seaweed
4 shiitake mushrooms (sliced, warmed in the dashi stock)
80g samphire (gently steamed)
60g rock shrimp (deep fried to crispy)
kale (few leaves, deep fried to crispy)
20 small florets Romanesco cauliflower (steamed)

Method

For The Dashi Stock (Prepare ahead)

Soak the kombu in spring water overnight and leave at room temperature.

Heat the water with the kombu to 60°C and hold the temperature for 1 hour. Remove the kombu, increase to 80°C, add the bonito flakes and soak until the bonito sinks to the bottom, about 30 seconds. Pass through a muslin, then add the sake. Season with the white soy sauce, yuzu juice and add salt to taste.

Chef's Tip

Concentrate on perfecting the dashi stock as this brings the whole dish together. This makes a lot but it freezes well.

For The Squid Ink Pasta Dough

Mix the egg, ink and salt in a food processor. Add the flour and blitz to breadcrumbs. Knead the dough on a floured surface until smooth. Cover with cling film and refrigerate for 30 minutes.

For The Crab Ravioli Filling

Blitz the lemon sole and salt quickly in a chilled food processor bowl. Drizzle in the cream until incorporated, then pass through a sieve. Season with pepper, fold in the crab meats and place in a piping bag. Chill.

Roll out the pasta dough in a pasta machine, folding over and putting it back through while bringing the thickness setting down to number 2. Cut the pasta sheet in two. Pipe 4 mounds of fish mousse onto one of the pasta sheets, then brush the other pasta sheet with water and place on top. Seal all around the mousse mounds pushing out any excess air. Cut out with a round cutter. Cook the ravioli in a pot of salted, simmering water until it floats, then refresh in ice water.

For The Hake

Place a piece of hake on each nori sheet. Cut off any excess of nori, leaving enough to completely roll the hake into cylindrical shapes with a bamboo sheet. Seal with a brush of water on the edges. Refrigerate until needed.

To Plate

Warm the dashi stock (do not boil), then add the cockles and mussels. Steam the hake for 8 minutes. Warm the ravioli in a pan of salted water. Sprinkle the seaweeds in the bottom of 4 large bowls and top with the ravioli.

Add the mussels, cockles, hot stock and shiitake mushrooms. Slice each hake fillet into 3, place in the bowls and dot with wasabi caviar. Finish with the remaining garnishes.

RHUBARB, GINGER CUSTARD & DOUGHNUTS

SERVES 4

 *Rustenberg Straw Wine, Stellenbosch
(South Africa)*

Ingredients

Rhubarb Juice

1kg forced rhubarb (diced)
125g caster sugar, 75ml grenadine

Rhubarb Jelly

400ml rhubarb juice
4 leaves gelatine (softened in cold water)

Rhubarb Sorbet

100ml water, 100g sugar, 300ml rhubarb juice
½ lemon (juice of, as required)

Rhubarb Cream

350g cream cheese, 100g clotted cream
100g caster sugar, 1½ tbsp plain flour
½ tsp vanilla extract, 2 tbsp grenadine
4 tbsp reserved rhubarb purée
1 whole free range egg, 1 egg yolk
½ lemon (juice of)

Poached Rhubarb

200g forced rhubarb (cut into 2½cm lengths)
50g caster sugar, 50ml grenadine

Ginger Custard

500ml full-fat milk, ½ vanilla pod
½ thumb stem ginger (diced)
60g crystallised ginger (diced)
100g caster sugar, 6 free range egg yolks
25g plain flour, 20g cornflour

Doughnuts

110ml full-fat milk (warmed)
7g dried yeast, 275g caster sugar
1 free range egg (beaten)
25g butter (melted)
220g strong flour (plus a little extra for kneading)
½ tsp salt

Garnish

red vein sorrel cress, rhubarb crisps

Method

For The Rhubarb Juice For Sorbet And Jelly (Prepare ahead)
Seal the ingredients in a vac pac bag. Cook in simmering water for 20-25 minutes until soft. Alternatively, heat the sugar and grenadine, then add the rhubarb. Poach until soft. Pass through a muslin cloth or jelly bag and keep all the juice. Reserve the purée for later use.

For The Rhubarb Jelly (Prepare ahead)
Bring the rhubarb juice to a simmer, remove from the heat and stir in the gelatine leaves. Set in a 1 litre dish in the fridge.

For The Rhubarb Sorbet (Prepare ahead)
Bring the sugar and water to the boil to make a sugar stock. Mix the rhubarb juice with 75ml of the sugar stock and season with the lemon juice. Taste and add more lemon juice or sugar stock as required. Chill and churn in an ice cream machine.

For The Rhubarb Cream
Preheat the oven to 180°C (fan).
Whizz all the ingredients in a blender and lay out on a baking tray. Bake for 35 minutes or until there is no wobble left. Blend until smooth. Place into a 1 litre tub and refrigerate until needed.

For The Poached Rhubarb
Vac pac all the ingredients and cook in a water bath on 70°C for 20 minutes or until cooked *al dente*. Alternatively, heat the sugar with the grenadine, then add the rhubarb. Poach until al dente. Set aside.

For The Ginger Custard
Slowly bring the milk, vanilla, ginger and crystallised ginger to the boil in a heavy-bottomed pan. Whisk the sugar and yolks until pale, then whisk in the flour and cornflour. Pass the hot milk through a sieve, then whisk into the egg sugar mix until smooth. Pour back into the pan. Bring the mix to the boil on a medium heat, whisking all the time. Chill. Transfer to a piping bag and reserve in the fridge.

For The Doughnuts
Activate the yeast with the milk and 25g of sugar. Mix all the ingredients, except the 250g of sugar, until smooth using a dough hook, kneading until it pushes back. Prove in a bowl covered with lightly oiled cling film until double the size. Portion the dough into 30g balls and leave to prove on a lightly floured tray.
Once risen to double the size, deep fry (170°C) until golden brown on one side, turn to fry on the other. Roll in the remaining sugar.

To Assemble
Place a *quenelle* of rhubarb cream and sorbet onto the plate. Pipe 2 small rounds of custard on the plate and into the doughnuts. Sit the doughnuts on top of the custard rounds. Cut out 12 cylinders of jelly and arrange 3 on each plate. Drain the poached rhubarb and add 4 pieces on each plate. Garnish with rhubarb crisps and red vein sorrel cress.

066
THE MASONS ARMS

Knowstone, South Molton, Devon, EX36 4RY

01398 341 231
www.masonsarmsdevon.co.uk Twitter: @MasonsKnowstone @markdodsonchef

Mark and Sarah Dodson's idyllic 13th Century, characterful thatched inn, with a cosy beamed bar and comfortable lounge, offers log fires and a warm welcome. For 12 years, Mark held the position of head chef at Michel Roux's Waterside Inn, at Bray. His food displays a modern take on British and French classics with a certain complexity to the cooking.

"We moved here in 2005 when we made a life changing decision to set up in Devon," says Mark. "The challenge was to make the pub exactly the kind of place that we would like to find if exploring Devon, with friendly service and first class food. We aim to serve good, honest food, locally sourced wherever possible and with equal care taken in every step from first preparation to final presentation. Sarah runs our front of house and, like every traditional local, you will soon feel relaxed and at home with our friendly staff."

The inn is set in the wonderful countryside of Exmoor and, weather permitting, you can also eat and drink outside whilst admiring the fantastic views.

Mark and Sarah naturally take great pride in their menus, which are always changing with the seasons, aiming to cater for everyone. They offer an extensive wine list to suit all tastes from France to the New World. Mark has more recently started masterclasses at the Masons Arms, and have become so popular, they are now a permanent monthly fixture.

The Masons Arms has been recognised by all the major guides and was awarded a Michelin Star in 2006 after only six months, which has been retained since. 2016 saw The Masons reach the top 10 of the Estrella UK Pub awards. Still proud to be the village local!

ARANCINI WITH BEETROOT THREE WAYS

SERVES 4

 Feudi di San Gregorio Albente Falanghina
(Italy)

Ingredients

Arancini
½ onion (finely chopped)
olive oil (splash of)
200g carnaroli rice
50ml white wine
375ml vegetable stock
50g Parmesan cheese (finely grated)
75ml double cream
90g mozzarella cheese (12 even cubes)
flour, egg (beaten)
breadcrumbs (to *pane*)

Horseradish Cream
80ml double cream
1 tsp creamed horseradish

Turned Beetroots
2 medium beetroots (peeled)
25g soft, light brown sugar
50ml red wine vinegar

Beetroot Purée
300g raw beetroot (peeled, roughly diced)
200ml double cream
seasoning

Pickled Beetroot
1 medium golden beetroot (enough for 12 good, round slices)
200ml white wine vinegar
100g sugar

Garnish
salad leaves or cress
horseradish (freshly grated)

Method

For The Arancini

Sweat the onion in a pan with a little oil, without colouring, until soft. Add the rice and stir to coat the grains in oil. Pour the white wine into the pan and bring to the boil without stirring. Add the vegetable stock, bit by bit, until the rice is cooked but with a little 'bite' remaining. Add both the Parmesan and the cream before bringing back to the boil. Season the mixture, then spread the risotto onto a tray. Refrigerate until cold.

Shape the rice around the cubes of mozzarella. Dust in the flour, egg wash and then the breadcrumbs. Deep fry at 170°C until golden. Drain and season.

For The Horseradish Cream

Bring the cream to the boil. Stir in a teaspoon of creamed horseradish, season and reserve.

For The Turned Beetroots

Cut each beetroot into 12 equal segments. Shape the segments with the aid of a sharp knife, turning them into barrel shapes to remove the hard edges.

Put the 24 turned beetroot barrels into a pan and cook with the sugar and vinegar, stirring occasionally. As the beetroots cook, the liquor will evaporate leaving a glaze on them.

For The Beetroot Purée

Cook the diced beetroots in lightly salted water on a low heat. Leave to cook until soft. This could take up to 2 hours and you may need to top up the water. When soft, drain well and return to the pan. Stir the beetroot around to evaporate the last of the liquid. Add the double cream, leave to cook and thicken. Once the mixture has thickened, place into a blender and blend until smooth. Season to taste, reserve and keep hot.

For The Pickled Beetroot

Peel and finely slice the beetroot.

Combine the sugar and vinegar in a pan and bring to the boil. Add the sliced beetroot, then leave them to cool in the pickling syrup.

To Serve

Make a swirl of purée on the plate. Dot around some of the horseradish cream. Place on the arancini, the 'turned' beetroots and the pickled beetroots (which can be rolled up). Garnish with some delicate salad leaves or cress. Finish with freshly grated horseradish.

> **Chef's Tip**
> A great way to use up left over risotto, the Italian equivalent of 'bubble and squeak'!

LOIN OF VENISON WITH POACHED PEAR & BLUE CHEESE GRATIN

SERVES 4

 A lovely Rhône wine such as a Gigondas (France)

Ingredients

600g venison loin (trimmed, portioned into 4 x 150g pieces - retain any bones and trimmings for the sauce)

Venison Sauce

venison bones and trimmings
2 carrots (chopped)
1 onion (chopped)
1 stick celery (chopped)
1 tbsp tomato purée
water (to cover)
2 tbsp pear poaching liquid

Blue Cheese Gratin

4 medium potatoes (peeled)
90ml full-fat milk
125ml double cream
3 cloves garlic
200g blue cheese (we use Gorgonzola)

Poached Pears

2 pears (peeled, halved, cored)
200ml red wine
100g sugar
1 stick cinnamon

To Serve

salsify
cavolo nero
baby carrots

Method

For The Venison Sauce (Prepare ahead)

Preheat the oven to 180°C.

Roast the bones and trimmings for 45 minutes until golden brown before transferring into a smaller pan with the vegetables. Add a spoonful of tomato purée, sweat again, then cover with water. Leave the mixture to cook slowly for 8 hours. Once cooked, pass through a fine sieve and reduce until a good sauce consistency is achieved. Just before serving, reduce a couple of spoonfuls of the pear poaching liquid and add to the sauce to give a little depth and sweetness.

For The Blue Cheese Gratin

Preheat the oven to 150°C.

Boil together the milk, cream, garlic and cheese. Slice the potatoes and position in a suitable dish, pass the liquid onto the slices. Cover the top of the dish with greaseproof paper and bake in the oven for 1-1½ hours. Halfway through cooking, press down on the potatoes to ensure the gratin is compact, the potato should have a good colour but be soft all the way through.

For The Poached Pears

Poach the pears in the red wine with sugar and the cinnamon stick until just cooked. Leave them to cool in the liquid.

To Serve

Cook the venison in a pan until pink and leave it to rest before slicing. Cook the vegetables as desired.

Arrange the meat on the plate with the vegetables and add a good piece of the gratin. Slice and fan the pear before finally pouring a little of the sauce around the dish.

Chef's Tip

Venison needn't be a strong meat. Take it off the bone and lightly cover it in olive oil. Place in a container with a few juniper berries and a bay leaf and store in the fridge for up to 5 days.

CHOCOLATE CHEESECAKE WITH PEANUT ICE CREAM

SERVES 8

 Californian Muscat
(USA)

Ingredients

Chocolate Cheesecake

60g digestive biscuits
60g Hob Nob biscuits
70g butter (melted)
75g sugar
3 egg yolks
1 leaf gelatine (softened in cold water)
275ml double cream
200g cream cheese (softened)
50g dark chocolate (melted)
120g milk chocolate (melted)

Peanut Ice Cream

275ml full-fat milk
275ml double cream
10g glucose
5 egg yolks
140g sugar
25g smooth peanut butter

Honeycomb

50g caster sugar
15g golden syrup
50ml glucose
5g bicarbonate of soda

To Serve

raspberry coulis
chocolate (melted)

8 ring moulds (7cm diameter)

Method

For The Chocolate Cheesecake

Pulse the biscuits in a food processor and bind together with the butter. Push into the moulds and place in the fridge.

Bring the sugar to the boil with a drop of water, then pour the liquid onto the egg yolks and whisk until light. Boil 50ml of the double cream and dissolve the gelatine into it. Add the warm cream to the yolks and continue whisking until cool. Stir in the cream cheese and both chocolates. Lightly whip the remaining cream and carefully stir this into the mixture. Spoon on top of the biscuit bases and leave to set for 2-3 hours in the fridge.

For The Peanut Ice Cream

Combine the milk and cream together with the glucose and bring to the boil. Pour the mixture onto the yolks, whisking constantly. Continue to cook, stirring continuously, until the mixture thickens and coats the back of a spoon. Once cooked, blend the peanut butter into the mix and pass through a fine sieve. Leave to cool, then churn in an ice cream machine. Freeze.

For The Honeycomb

Boil together the sugar, syrup and glucose. Add the bicarbonate of soda and watch it grow! Pour onto a baking sheet and leave to cool. Break into small pieces.

To Serve

De-mould the cheesecake and gently place onto a plate. Decorate with a brush of chocolate, some raspberry coulis, the honeycomb and lastly the ice cream.

Chef's Tip

Amazing with caramelised bananas!

ORESTONE MANOR
HOTEL & RESTAURANT

Rock House Lane, Maidencombe, Torquay, TQ1 4SX

01803 897 511
www.orestonemanor.com Twitter: @Orestonemanor

A truly special place to stay, Orestone Manor is an elegant Georgian manor house perched on the hillside of the pretty little South Devon coastal town of Maidencombe. The hotel enjoys far reaching sea views over Lyme Bay and beyond.

The local area seems to have its own microclimate and Orestone Manor's sun terrace, surrounded by palm trees and lush gardens, has to be one of the finest spots of the English Riviera.

The Manor has a rich history, boasting associations with none other than legendary engineer Isambard Kingdom Brunel and his brother-in-law, painter John Caldicott Horsley. Today, the hotel is passionately owned and run by the D'Allen family and, as to be expected from a hotel run by two chefs, food is at the heart of the Orestone experience.

Afternoon tea at the hotel is a popular extravagance for locals. In winter the regulars sit snug by the fire tucking into cakes, but as soon as spring blooms, the indulgence moves to the terrace.

With 14 character bedrooms (two more have just been added due to demand), Orestone is a hugely popular short break destination.

Whilst the bedrooms are effortlessly luxurious, a stay at Orestone wouldn't be complete without sampling the exquisite dining offered by head chef Nathan Hill and his team, recognised with 2 AA Rosettes.

After dinner, guests can enjoy a tipple in the swanky new Brunel bar or retire to the various lounge areas in a comfy armchair. Heaven.

Set in the South Devon village of Maidencombe, Orestone Manor is a renowned luxury hotel and restaurant with stunning sea views. Owned and run by chefs, Orestone is a foodie heaven with a 2 AA Rosette award-winning restaurant.

Orestone Manor

—HOTEL & RESTAURANT—

★★★★

Luxury Accommodation • Award winning Restaurant
Fabulous Sun terrace • Spectacular Sea Views
Lunch • Dinner • Afternoon Tea

DUCK & PISTACHIO TERRINE, PLUM PUREE, APPLE & TRUFFLE SALAD

SERVES 4

 Château du Grand Caumont Corbières Cuvée Tradition, Languedoc-Roussillon (France)

Ingredients

Duck And Pistachio Terrine

4 duck legs
30g rock salt
1 tbsp black peppercorns (crushed)
4 cloves garlic (finely chopped)
2 bay leaves
4 sprigs thyme (chopped)
800g duck fat (melted, to cover)
4 red plums (sliced)
100g butter (melted)
50g pistachio nuts (shelled, peeled, toasted)
sugar (sprinkling of)

Duck Dressing

50ml brandy
100ml port
170g shallots (chopped)
4 sprigs thyme
1 clove garlic
250ml chicken stock

Plum Purée

8 red plums
2 tsp port
100g butter
1 stick cinnamon

Apple And Truffle Salad

1 green apple (diced)
micro herbs
white truffle shavings

Garnish

brioche (toasted)
sugared pistachio nuts
wild garlic flowers

loaf tin (lined with cling film)

Method

To Prepare The Duck (Prepare 36 hours ahead)

Combine the salt, pepper, garlic, bay and thyme and rub over the duck legs. Wrap in cling film and refrigerate for 24 hours.

Preheat the oven to 140°C (fan).

Rinse the legs then pat dry. Place them in a roasting tray, cover with the duck fat and bring up to 85°C. Transfer to the oven and cook uncovered for 2½ hours.

Remove from the oven and allow to cool in the cooking fat. When cool enough to handle, pick the meat from the bones and shred.

For The Duck Dressing

Combine all ingredients in a pan and bring up to the boil. Simmer to reduce by two thirds and leave to cool. Strain the mixture and pour the dressing over the shredded duck meat.

To Make The Duck And Pistachio Terrine

Blanch the plum slices quickly in boiling water, then dip them in melted butter. Cover the bottom of the loaf tin with a layer of plums. Add half of the duck meat and press down, until about 3cm thick. Scatter the toasted pistachio nuts on top and cover with the remaining duck meat, pressing down firmly, to a maximum depth of 7cm. Press with a weight in the fridge until cool.

For The Plum Purée

Cook all the ingredients over a medium heat, stirring occasionally to crush the plums, until they become very tender. Carefully remove the stones and blitz in a food processor. Pass through a *chinois* using a spoon to press the flesh through. Adjust the sweetness level if needed. It should be slightly tart in flavour.

For The Apple And Truffle Salad

Carefully combine the ingredients just prior to serving.

To Serve

Remove the terrine from the mould. Cut into slices, sprinkle with sugar and caramelise the plum top with a blow torch. Arrange with the fruit purée, then add the apple and truffle salad as pictured. Finish with sugared pistachio nuts and serve with toasted brioche.

Chef's Tip

Buy ready *confit* duck legs to save time. Apple can be substituted for the plum purée and terrine topping.

NOISETTE OF LAMB, HERB CRUST, NAVET PUREE, WILD GARLIC, POMME FONDANT, ROSEMARY JUS

SERVES 4

 Reserve du Couvent, Château Ksara, Bekaa Valley (Lebanon)

Ingredients

Noisette Of Lamb
2 prepared racks of lamb, 8 tbsp olive oil
2 sprigs rosemary (needles removed, chopped)
4 cloves garlic (roughly chopped)

Rosemary Jus
3 tbsp fresh rosemary (chopped)
2 tbsp shallots (chopped), 1 tbsp garlic (crushed)
½ tsp salt, ½ tsp ground black pepper
130ml lamb stock, 130ml veal or beef stock
130ml ruby port

Navet Purée
1kg turnips (peeled, roughly chopped)
3 cloves garlic (peeled), 350ml double cream
50g butter, seasoning

Fondant Potatoes
4 large potatoes (cut into rounds using a
cookie cutter)
butter (knob of)
75ml chicken or vegetable stock
2 cloves garlic (crushed)
3 sprigs fresh thyme, seasoning

Heritage Carrots
500g heritage carrots (cut into barrel shapes)
1 tsp sugar, ½ tsp salt , 6 sprigs thyme, 50g butter

Wild Garlic
240g wild garlic leaves
butter (knob of), seasoning

Herb Dust
100g panko breadcrumbs
3 tbsp mixed fresh herbs (chopped)

Garnish
wild garlic flowers

Method

For The Noisette Of Lamb (Prepare 24 hours ahead)
Mix together the olive oil, rosemary and garlic and smother the mixture over the lamb joints. Marinate overnight in the fridge.

Chef's Tip
Ask your butcher to prepare 2 racks of lamb; boned out loin of lamb from racks wrapped in the fat from the rack, then tied into cylindrical joints.

For The Rosemary Jus
Add the dry ingredients to a pan on a high heat for 30 seconds. Pour in the stocks and port and bring to the boil. Simmer until reduced by half, then pass through a *chinois*. Return to a clean pan and reduce further to adjust the consistency if needed.

For The Navet Purée
Boil the turnips in plenty of water until very tender. Drain, then return to the pot. Add the garlic and heat until dry for 2 minutes. Mix in the cream and butter. Blitz in a food processor until smooth. Pass the mixture through a *chinois* using a spoon to push it through. Season to taste and add extra cream if the consistency needs adjusting.

For The Fondant Potatoes
Fry the potato rounds on each side in butter until golden brown. Add the stock, garlic, herbs and seasoning. Simmer with a lid on until they become tender. Remove from the stock.

For The Heritage Carrots
Place the carrots in a pan with enough water to just cover them. Add the sugar, salt, thyme and butter. Bring to the boil, then simmer until the water has evaporated.

For The Wild Garlic
Gently wilt the wild garlic with a little water, butter and seasoning in a shallow frying pan for 1 minute.

For The Herb Dust
Blitz the panko breadcrumbs with mixed herbs in a blender until it becomes a green-coloured powder.

To Assemble The Dish
Preheat the oven to 200°C (fan).
Season and seal the lamb in a hot pan until golden. Transfer to the oven and cook for 15 minutes. This will give you a pink lamb. Leave for longer if you prefer. Roll in the herb dust and leave to rest for at least 10 minutes. Return the lamb to a hot oven for another 2-3 minutes just before carving. Serve as pictured.

DUCK EGG CUSTARD TART, APPLE PUREE, CINNAMON ICE CREAM

SERVES 8

Somerset Pomona Cider, Brandy Liqueur
(UK)

Ingredients

Sweet Pastry

90g butter
65g caster sugar
200g plain flour
3 free-range egg yolks

Duck Egg Custard Filling

6 duck egg yolks
100g caster sugar
500ml double cream
¼ whole nutmeg (grated)

Apple Purée

3 Granny Smith apples (peeled, cored, thinly sliced)
100g butter

Cinnamon Ice Cream

250ml double cream
250ml full-fat milk
2 sticks cinnamon
6 egg yolks
200g caster sugar

25-30cm metal tart case (greased, floured)

Method

For The Sweet Pastry

Mix the butter, sugar and flour to create a breadcrumb texture.

Add in the yolks and mix well. Remove the mixture from the bowl and gently knead to form a dough ball. Rest in the fridge for 20 minutes, covered with cling film.

Preheat the oven to 170°C (fan).

Roll out the pastry to a pound coin thickness.

Line the tin with the pastry and blind bake until crisp, about 30 minutes. Set aside to cool.

For The Duck Egg Custard Filling

Preheat the oven to 100°C (fan).

Whisk together the egg yolks and caster sugar. Heat the cream until it starts to boil, then add slowly to the egg mixture, whisking continuously. Pass through a fine sieve, skimming off any foam.

Pour the custard mixture into the baked pastry case. Grate a generous amount of nutmeg on the top. Bake for 40-50 minutes until just set. Allow to cool and refrigerate.

For The Apple Purée

Cook the thinly sliced apple in melted butter until soft. Blend to a smooth purée.

To Make The Cinnamon Ice Cream

Heat the cream, milk and cinnamon in a pan.

Mix the egg yolks with the sugar in a bowl.

When the cream mixture reaches the boil, carefully whisk into the egg and sugar. Allow to cool, then remove the cinnamon sticks.

Churn in an ice cream machine.

Chef's Tip

Try pairing with other ice creams such as rhubarb ripple.

To Plate

Remove the tart from the fridge 1 hour before serving. Slice with a warm knife and arrange on the plate with the other elements as pictured.

086
OUTLAW'S FISH KITCHEN

1 Middle Street, Port Isaac, Cornwall, PL29 3RH

01208 881 183
www.outlaws.co.uk/fishkitchen Twitter: @Fish_Kitchen

Outlaw's Fish Kitchen boasts 1 Michelin star and is proud of its reputation for being a fun place for seafood lovers to dine. Housed in a tiny, former fisherman's cottage at the top of the slipway, customers are able to see the fishermen bringing in their catch when the tide is right. It truly is a place to enjoy the freshest fish and seafood whilst also experiencing a sense of what this historical fishing port is all about.

Here, head chef Tim Barnes, who trained in the Restaurant Nathan Outlaw kitchen under Nathan and Chris, heads a small team. Front of house, locally born Megan Rees and her team extend a warm welcome to customers, delighting in making their visit an experience to remember. Outlaw's Fish Kitchen offers both lunch and dinner service, opening throughout the week during the summer.

At Outlaw's Fish Kitchen, small, delicious plates of fish and seafood are cooked to order and served when ready. The menu is dictated by the catch that day so it is ever changing. Here, customers are able to choose as many or as few plates as they wish, often opting to share and thus having a taste of everything on offer!

The décor in the restaurant is pleasantly rustic and in keeping with the surroundings. Its cool tones and scrubbed tables give a sense of the history gone before. Completed by low ceilings and beams, it's easy for customers to imagine what life would have been like in bygone times.

Food photography by David Loftus

Situated in a tiny, former fisherman's cottage at the top of the harbour slipway, Michelin starred Outlaw's Fish Kitchen offers small plates of delicious fish and seafood.

CRISPY FRIED GREY MULLET, CHILLI JAM

SERVES 4 AS A STARTER (or up to 8 as a bite)

 Kung Fu Girl Riesling 2014, Charles Smith,
Washington State (USA)

Ingredients

Chilli Jam

1 red onion (peeled, finely diced)
4 red peppers (cored, deseeded, finely sliced)
6 red chillies (deseeded, finely sliced)
3 garlic cloves (peeled, chopped)
400g tin plum tomatoes
300g soft brown sugar
150ml red wine vinegar
2 lemongrass stalks (tough outer layers removed,
finely chopped)
salt (pinch of)

Crispy Fried Grey Mullet

400g grey mullet fillet (skinned, pin-boned)
2 tbsp coriander (chopped)
1 lime (finely grated zest of)
½ tsp ground cumin
½ tsp cayenne pepper
100g gluten-free or plain flour
120ml Cornish Pilsner (or similar beer)
sunflower oil (for deep frying)
sea salt and freshly ground black pepper

To Serve

2 limes (halved)

Method

For The Chilli Jam

Place all of the ingredients into a heavy-bottomed pan (I use a cast-iron one). Bring to the boil, stirring to dissolve the sugar. Lower the heat and simmer gently, stirring occasionally, for about 45 minutes until the jam is well reduced. Once it starts to catch on the bottom of the pan, stir constantly over the heat until it looks like bubbling lava. Transfer to a bowl and leave to cool. Once cooled, the jam can be kept in the fridge in a sealed container.

For The Crispy Fried Grey Mullet

Cut the mullet into roughly 4cm chunks. Mix the coriander, lime zest, cumin, cayenne and a good pinch of salt together in a bowl. Add the mullet pieces and toss to mix. Leave to marinate for 30 minutes.

Mix the flour and beer together until smooth to make the batter. Heat the oil in a deep-fat fryer or other suitable deep, heavy-bottomed pan to 180°C. Season the fish with salt and pepper.

You will need to cook the fish in 2 or 3 batches. One at a time, dip each chunk into the batter to coat, then carefully lower into the hot oil. Deep fry for 3-4 minutes until cooked and crispy. Gently lift the fish out and drain on kitchen paper. Keep warm while you cook the rest.

To Serve

Sprinkle the fish chunks with a little salt and spear onto cocktail sticks. Serve immediately on a platter or individual plates with a bowl of chilli jam and lime wedges on the side.

Chef's Tip

I serve these crisp-fried fish bites on cocktail sticks on a platter with a dish of chilli jam. They are great as a pre-dinner bite, or handed around at a party. You'll probably have more chilli jam than you need, but it will keep for ages in the fridge in a sealed container and is delicious with cheese and cold meats.

BEER-CURED SALMON WITH CUCUMBER & SEAWEED SALAD

SERVES 4

🍷 *Saint-Bris Vieilles Vignes 2012, Clotilde Davenne*
Burgundy (France)

Ingredients

Beer-Cured Salmon

500g very fresh wild or organic farmed salmon
(trimmed, skinned)
100g sea salt
100g soft brown sugar
150ml strong beer (I use Sharps Honey Spiced IPA)

Cucumber And Seaweed Salad

100ml olive oil
70ml light rapeseed oil
50ml white wine vinegar
1 large shallot (peeled, finely chopped)
2 tsp mixed seaweed flakes
sea salt
1 large cucumber

Salad Cream

2 egg yolks
2 tsp English mustard
2 tsp caster sugar
2 tbsp lemon juice
100ml rapeseed oil
150ml double cream

To Garnish

1 tbsp dried seaweed flakes

Method

To Cure The Salmon (Prepare ahead)

Lay the fish on a tray and sprinkle evenly with the salt and sugar. Turn the fish over in the cure a few times to ensure it is coated all over. Drizzle evenly with the beer, then wrap the whole tray in cling film and place in the fridge to cure for 6 hours.

Unwrap the fish, wash off the cure with cold water and pat dry with kitchen paper. Wrap the fish tightly in fresh cling film and place back in the fridge for 1 hour to firm up.

For The Cucumber And Seaweed Salad

Put the oils and wine vinegar into a pan with the shallot, seaweed and a pinch of salt. Bring to a simmer over a medium heat and let bubble for 2 minutes. Remove from the heat and allow to cool.

Meanwhile, peel and thinly slice the cucumber. Lay the cucumber slices in a dish and pour the cooled liquor over them. Cover with cling film, pushing it down onto the surface to keep the cucumber fully submerged. Leave to stand for at least an hour.

For The Salad Cream

Whisk the egg yolks, mustard, sugar and lemon juice together in a bowl for 1 minute, then gradually whisk in the oil, a little at a time, until fully incorporated. To finish, slowly whisk in the cream and season with salt to taste. Cover and refrigerate until required.

To Serve

Slice the cured salmon into 3cm thick pieces and divide between 4 plates.

Drain off some of the liquor and the shallots from the cucumber. Add a pile of cucumber salad to each plate and spoon over the cucumber liquor. Dress the plates with salad cream and seaweed flakes. Serve at room temperature.

Chef's Tip

Salmon has the perfect texture and balance of oiliness for curing. I like to experiment with different cures and this combination of beer and seaweed is something I came up with for a charity dinner.

RHUBARB SPONGE, ALMOND CREAM & LEMON CREME FRAICHE

SERVES 8

 Pink Bug Juice, Rinaldi, Piedmont (Italy)

Ingredients

Rhubarb Sponge

2 vanilla pods (split lengthways)
225g unsalted butter
225g egg whites (5-6 large eggs)
225g caster sugar
90g ground almonds
90g plain flour
8 pieces rhubarb (about 10cm long)

Almond Cream

90g ground almonds
65g caster sugar
300ml full-fat milk
1 vanilla pod (split lengthways)

Baked Rhubarb

1kg rhubarb (cut into 8-10cm pieces)
1 orange (juice and microplaned zest of)
250g caster sugar
100ml water

Lemon Crème Fraîche

600ml full-fat crème fraîche
100g icing sugar
1 lemon (juice and grated zest of)

8 moulds (8cm x 4cm, lined with baking parchment)

Method

For The Rhubarb Sponge

Scrape the seeds from the vanilla pods and set aside. Put the pods into a saucepan with the butter and place over a medium heat. When the butter has melted and starts to brown, remove from the heat and allow to cool. Discard the vanilla pod.

Preheat the oven to 200°C.

Whisk the egg whites and sugar together in a large bowl for 1 minute. Add the ground almonds, flour and vanilla seeds and mix well. Whisk in the brown butter, ensuring it is all incorporated. Pour the mixture into the prepared moulds. Lay the 8 rhubarb pieces on top of the mixture and bake for 12–14 minutes. To check if the sponges are cooked, insert a small knife into the centre of one; if it comes out clean, they are ready.

For The Almond Cream

Put the ground almonds, sugar and milk into a heavy-bottomed pan with the vanilla. Place over a medium heat and cook, stirring often, until thickened; this will take about 15 minutes. Remove from the heat, discard the vanilla pod and cover the surface with cling film to stop a skin forming.

For The Baked Rhubarb

Preheat the oven to 200°C.

Put the rhubarb, orange zest and juice, sugar and the water into a deep roasting tray. Cook in the oven until the rhubarb is soft, about 10 minutes. Remove from the oven and leave to cool in the liquid.

For The Lemon Crème Fraîche

Whisk the crème fraîche, icing sugar, lemon zest and juice together in a bowl. Cover and refrigerate until needed.

To Serve

Turn out the sponges and place in shallow bowls. Serve warm with the baked rhubarb, almond cream and lemon crème fraîche on the side.

Chef's Tip

More like a French financier or Madeleine than a traditional sponge, this is a versatile recipe that can take all manner of spices and pretty much any fruit. Rhubarb is one of my favourite fruits to bake and is delicious with the almond cream and sponge.

096
RESTAURANT NATHAN OUTLAW

6 New Road, Port Isaac, Cornwall, PL29 3SB

01208 880 896
www.nathan-outlaw.com/restaurant Twitter: @ResNathanOutlaw

Restaurant Nathan Outlaw is the 2 Michelin starred flagship of Nathan's business. It first opened in Fowey, then moved to the St Enodoc Hotel in Rock and finally relocated to Port Isaac in March 2015, when Nathan and his wife Rachel took sole charge. This is the restaurant where Nathan can be found in the kitchen most of the time.

The restaurant team is one that has been built up over the years. Stephi Little and Anna Davey are responsible for the smooth running of front of house whilst Stephi's husband, Damon, is Nathan's immensely knowledgeable sommelier. In the kitchen, Chris Simpson, who has worked with Nathan for over 10 years and is an excellent chef in his own right, is head chef.

The restaurant offers a seafood and fish tasting menu only, although a superb vegetarian menu can be provided with prior notice. All the seafood offered here is caught around the Cornish coast and from fishermen using responsible fishing methods. Most of the vegetables and other items on the menu are also sourced within a few miles.

The restaurant is furnished in a modern and comfortable style, with polished wood floors and panoramic views across the bay. The restaurant also showcases a number of paintings and other pieces by local artists, mostly with a theme befitting a seafood restaurant. Nathan's own tastes are reflected throughout, even down to the music, which he mixes personally.

Food photography by David Loftus

The Flagship of Nathan's restaurant business - Restaurant Nathan Outlaw holds 2 Michelin stars, 4 AA Rosettes and ranked fourth in the Waitrose Good Food Guide's 'Top 50 Restaurants of 2016' in the UK.

ph by Stephen Perez

CRAB PATE WITH PINK GRAPEFRUIT

SERVES 4 AS A STARTER

Demi-Sec 2012, Camel Valley
Cornwall (UK)

Ingredients

300g white crab meat (picked)
sea salt and freshly ground black pepper

Crab Pâté

200g brown crab meat
30ml brandy
cayenne pepper (pinch of)
ground cumin (pinch of)
200ml double cream
1½ sheets bronze leaf gelatine (soaked in cold water)
2 tbsp lime juice
sea salt (pinch of)

Pink Grapefruit Jelly

300ml freshly squeezed pink grapefruit juice (from about 2 grapefruit)
50g caster sugar
sea salt (pinch of)
2½ sheets bronze leaf gelatine (soaked in cold water)

To Garnish

1 pink grapefruit (segmented)
mustard cress

To Serve

sourdough bread

4 ramekins

Method

For The White Crab Meat

Pick through your crab meat, checking for any shell or cartilage to discard. Put the white crab meat into a bowl and season with salt and pepper to taste, then divide it equally between 4 small bowls or ramekins.

For The Crab Pâté (Prepare ahead)

Heat the brown crab meat, brandy and spices in a small pan over a low heat. Simmer gently for 1 minute, then add the cream and heat through.

Squeeze out the excess water from the gelatine, then add it to the brown crab, off the heat. Transfer to a blender and blend for 1 minute, adding the lime juice and a pinch of salt. Pass the mixture through a sieve into a jug and pour it equally over the white crab meat in the bowls. Place in the fridge to set for approximately 2 hours.

For The Pink Grapefruit Jelly

Put the grapefruit juice, sugar and a pinch of salt into a pan and bring to the boil. Squeeze the excess water from the gelatine, then add to the juice mixture, off the heat, stirring until fully melted. Leave to cool, but don't let it set.

Pour the cooled, liquid jelly evenly on top of the set crab pâté and return to the fridge to set for 1 hour.

To Serve

Remove the ramekins from the fridge around 20 minutes before serving to bring to room temperature. Cut away the peel and pith from the grapefruit and cut out the segments from between the membranes. Garnish the pâté with the grapefruit segments and cress and add a drizzle of olive oil. Toast the sourdough and serve with the pâté.

Chef's Tip

For this beautiful starter, make sure your crab meat is in tip-top condition as the dish really shows off its quality. Trust me, you will get a few wows when your guests, family and friends try it. I like to serve it with a pile of lightly toasted sourdough.

RAW SCALLOPS, CELERIAC BROTH & GREEN CHILLI

SERVES 4 AS A STARTER

 Trevannion 2013, Knightor Winery Cornwall (UK)

Ingredients

12 very fresh scallops (shelled, cleaned, roes removed)

Green Chilli Oil

30g coriander (leaves picked)
300ml light olive oil
2 green chillies (chopped, seeds left in)

Celeriac Broth

1 large or 2 small celeriac (peeled, diced)
sunflower oil (drizzle of)

Celeriac Pickle

½ celeriac (peeled, cut into matchsticks)
75ml cider
75ml cider vinegar
75ml water
75g caster sugar
salt (pinch of)
coriander leaves (handful of, picked)

Celeriac Crisps

½ celeriac (peeled)
sunflower oil (for deep frying)

To Finish And Serve

lemon juice (a good squeeze of)
sea salt
1-2 green chillies (deseeded, finely chopped)

Method

For The Green Chilli Oil (Prepare the day before)
Blanch the coriander in a pan of boiling, salted water for 30 seconds, then lift out and plunge into a bowl of cold water to refresh. Drain and squeeze out the excess water, then place in a blender. Add the olive oil and chillies and blitz for 5 minutes. Pour into a container and place in the fridge for 24 hours. Decant just before serving.

For The Celeriac Broth
Weigh the diced celeriac and note the weight. Heat a pan (large enough to hold the celeriac comfortably) and add a drizzle of oil. Add the celeriac and cook over a medium heat until caramelised all over, at least 20 minutes. Add the same volume of water as the weight of the celeriac and bring to the boil. Lower the heat and simmer for 20 minutes.

Strain the liquid into a clean pan. (Save the celeriac for a stew or mash with your next meal). Bring the liquor to a simmer and let bubble until reduced to about 150ml; it should be a lovely, golden brown colour. Strain again and allow to cool. Cover and refrigerate until required.

For The Celeriac Pickle
Place the celeriac matchsticks in a bowl. Heat the cider, vinegar, water, sugar and a pinch of salt in a small pan to dissolve the sugar and bring to the boil. Pour over the celeriac, cover and let cool.

For The Celeriac Crisps
Slice the celeriac thinly on a mandolin. Heat the oil in a deep-fat fryer or other suitable deep, heavy pan to 150°C. Line a tray with kitchen paper. Fry the celeriac slices in batches; lower into the hot oil and fry until golden all over. Remove with a strainer, drain on kitchen paper and sprinkle with sea salt. Allow to cool.

To Finish And Serve
Drain the pickled celeriac and toss the coriander through it. On a clean board with a sharp knife, slice the scallops in half horizontally and season with a little salt.

Share the scallops and celeriac pickle between 4 plates or shallow bowls. Warm the broth gently in a small pan and add salt and lemon juice to taste. Spoon the broth equally into the dishes and finish with the celeriac crisps, a drizzle of green chilli oil and a sprinkling of chillies. Serve immediately.

Chef's Tip

Raw scallops always go down really well when we serve them in the restaurants so I wanted to share a favourite recipe of mine here. Make it during autumn and winter, when celeriac is at its best. I make a stock and a pickle from the celeriac and finish the dish with celeriac crisps and a drizzle of chilli oil.

PASSION FRUIT & TOASTED COCONUT ICE CREAM SANDWICH

SERVES 4

 Eisrébe 2014, Joseph Phelps
California (USA)

Ingredients

Passion Fruit Ice Cream

300ml fresh passion fruit juice (from about
15-20 passion fruit)
400ml double cream
5 medium egg yolks
120g caster sugar
3 sheets bronze leaf gelatine (soaked in cold water)
260g cream cheese (room temperature)

Coconut Biscuit

55g desiccated coconut
100g egg whites (about 3 medium eggs)
100g caster sugar
100g plain flour

Coconut Yoghurt

50g desiccated coconut
300ml full-fat Greek yoghurt
1 lime (finely grated zest of)
30g icing sugar

Passion Fruit Syrup

80ml passion fruit (from about 4-5 passion fruit)
50g caster sugar

6 x 7½cm square moulds

Method

For The Passion Fruit Ice Cream (Prepare ahead)
Pour the passion fruit juice into a large pan and bring to a simmer over a medium heat. Let it bubble and reduce by three quarters, then take off the heat.

Add the cream to the reduced passion fruit juice and return to a simmer. Meanwhile, whisk the eggs and sugar together in a bowl. Pour on the hot passion fruit cream, whisking as you do so. While it is still very hot, squeeze the excess water from the gelatine, then add to the mixture, whisking to dissolve. Let cool, then cover and refrigerate until cold.

Once the mixture is cold, whisk in the cream cheese. Put the mixture into a piping bag and pipe into 6 individual moulds. Freeze until firm for roughly 4-5 hours or preferably overnight.

For The Coconut Biscuit (Prepare ahead)
Preheat the oven to 180°C and the grill to medium-high.
Scatter the desiccated coconut on a grill tray and grill until golden, stirring every 2 minutes to colour evenly. Let cool.

Whisk the egg whites and sugar together in a bowl until evenly mixed. Add the cooled, toasted coconut and flour and stir to combine. Using a palette knife, spread the mixture thinly and evenly on a baking tray lined with a silicone mat. Bake for 8–10 minutes until golden all over.

When you take the tray from the oven, mark your desired biscuit shapes with a sharp knife. Once cooled, they should snap where marked, with a little help. Keep in an airtight container until ready to assemble.

For The Coconut Yoghurt (not pictured)
Toast the coconut as above and let cool. Once cooled, add to the yoghurt with the lime zest and icing sugar and stir until evenly combined. Set aside in the fridge until ready to serve.

For The Passion Fruit Syrup
Heat the passion fruit juice and sugar in a pan over a medium heat to dissolve the sugar. Bring to a simmer, lower the heat slightly and cook until reduced to a syrupy consistency. Leave to cool.

To Assemble
De-mould the ice creams and sandwich each one between 2 coconut biscuits. Serve immediately, with the passion fruit syrup spooned over and a dollop of coconut yoghurt on the side.

Chef's Tip

This recipe is inspired by nostalgic memories of ice cream sandwiches my mum would make with Neapolitan ice cream bought from the ice cream man. I'd like to think it's an improvement!

ROSEWARNE MANOR RESTAURANT

Gwinear Road, Connor Downs, Hayle, Cornwall, TR27 5JQ

01209 610 414
www.rosewarnemanor.co.uk Twitter: @RosewarneManor

Surrounded by lush Cornish countryside, yet just minutes away from glorious beaches, Rosewarne Manor is a haven away from the summer crowds. Enjoy looking out over the large gardens with their mature trees and shrubs whilst dining in a relaxed and welcoming atmosphere. This is a place where you can enjoy good food and feel completely at ease. The service is efficient but also reflects the relaxed ambience that is so typical of Cornwall, and so often keenly sought out by visitors.

Rosewarne Manor, owned by Cyril and Gill Eustice, has two main dining rooms as well as a wood panelled private dining room that seats 12. All have excellent garden views and are flooded with natural light. In the summer months, the patio provides the opportunity for al fresco dining in the lovely Cornish air. The dress code is distinctly informal.

The restaurant offers an extensively stocked bar, including draught lagers and local ales, providing a wide choice.

The menu features the very best of Cornish meat and line caught fish. Choice is also evident on the menu where the 2 AA Rosette award-winning à la carte is complemented by a high quality bar and steak menu. Here no one will frown or raise their eyebrows if your group choose from both menus. If you are seeking something truly special, then book in for one of the tasting menu evenings.

Head chef Phil Thomas and the Rosewarne team have built a reputation for fine food and championed the use of local fresh produce leading to four Taste of the West Gold awards, 2 AA Rosettes, a Platinum CHEFS award and Bridal Excellence trophy.

CORNISH BLUE CHEESE PANNA COTTA WITH GINGER FAIRINGS & APPLE TEXTURES

SERVES 8

 Camel Valley Bacchus Dry, Cornwall (England)

Ingredients

Cornish Blue Cheese Panna Cotta

250ml double cream
250ml full-fat milk
75ml white wine
1 banana shallot (finely chopped)
250g Cornish blue cheese
4 leaves gelatine (soaked in cold water)
¼ tsp nutmeg
¼ tsp white pepper

Cornish Ginger Fairings

450g plain flour
salt (pinch of)
2 tsp mixed spice
1 tsp cinnamon
2 tsp ground ginger
4 tsp baking powder
4 tsp bicarbonate of soda
240g butter
100g caster sugar
8 tbsp golden syrup

Burnt Apple Purée

6 Braeburn apples (skin on, cored, quartered)
1 tsp cinnamon
4 tbsp caster sugar
½ tsp mixed spice

Roast Apple Pieces

2 Braeburn apples (peeled, cored)
50g unsalted butter
2 tbsp caster sugar

Garnish

red vein sorrel
apple blossom flowers

8 ramekins

Method

For The Cornish Blue Cheese Panna Cotta

Heat together the cream, milk, wine, shallot and blue cheese, gently simmering until the shallot is soft. Squeeze out any excess water from the gelatine and add it to the warm mix. Liquidise the mixture and pass it through a sieve. Season with nutmeg and pepper before pouring into the moulds to set.

For The Cornish Ginger Fairings

Preheat the oven to 190°C.

Sift the flour, salt, spices, baking powder and bicarbonate together. Rub in the butter and add the sugar. Heat the syrup and add to the mix. Knead the mixture to create a stiff dough, then roll it into a sheet approximately 6mm thick. Bake for 8 minutes until golden. Leave to cool.

For The Burnt Apple Purée

Preheat the oven to 200°C.

Place the apple quarters onto a non-stick baking tray and sprinkle the other ingredients on top. Roast in the oven until blackened, but still slightly soft, about 45 minutes. Whilst still warm, pass through a fine sieve to give a dark brown purée.

For The Roast Apple Pieces

Finely dice the apples. Pan fry in the melted butter and sugar until soft. Set aside and allow to cool.

To Serve

Remove the blue cheese panna cottas from the moulds and carefully roll them in some of the crushed ginger fairings. Pipe some large dots of the spiced apple purée around the plate. Garnish with roast apple pieces, red vein sorrel and apple blossom flowers. Finish with crumbled ginger fairing pieces.

Chef's Tip

The blue cheese mousse could easily be used as a savoury cheesecake!

CAERHAYS CORNISH ESTATE VENISON, BITTERSWEET CHOCOLATE BLACK PUDDING, LITTLE GEM LETTUCE, ORANGE & VANILLA

SERVES 4

 *Jarrah Wood Shiraz
(Australia)*

Ingredients

500g venison loin (trimmed)
2 little gem lettuce

Bittersweet Chocolate Black Pudding

500g dried pig's blood (available online)
25ml sherry vinegar
50ml cream sherry
200g pork back fat
10g sea salt
2 large banana shallots (finely chopped)
80ml double cream
100g pearl barley (cooked)
100g breadcrumbs
100g 70% dark chocolate (chopped)

Orange And Vanilla Reduction

1 litre pure orange juice
300ml brown chicken stock
250g unsalted butter
2 vanilla pods (scraped)

Butternut Squash Purée

1 large butternut squash (peeled, roughly chopped)
1 tsp mixed spice

Method

For The Bittersweet Chocolate Black Pudding

Add the vinegar and sherry to the pig's blood. Render half of the back fat and strain to remove the solids.

Use the rendered back fat to sweat down the shallots until soft. Remove the pan from the heat, add the cream and the remaining back fat, season with salt. Add this to the pig's blood mixture along with pearl barley, breadcrumbs and chocolate. Roll tightly in cling film to form a sausage shape, tie each end. Steam for 25-30 minutes, set aside to cool.

Chef's Tip

Make twice as much of the black pudding because it is gorgeous!

For The Orange And Vanilla Reduction

Combine the orange juice, chicken stock, butter and vanilla seeds and pods in a large pan. Bring the mixture to the boil, then reduce down to the thickness of double cream. Strain to remove the vanilla pods and set aside.

For The Butternut Squash Purée

Preheat the oven to 190°C.

Roast the chopped squash for 40 minutes until tender. Reserve some diced roast squash to garnish. Blend the rest with the mixed spice until smooth and season to taste.

For The Venison And Little Gem Lettuce

Pan fry the venison loin for 5 minutes on a medium-high heat. Set aside to rest.

Slice the black pudding into 10mm pieces. Grill both sides until warmed through.

Trim the lettuce, ensuring the stems are clean. Pan fry over a high heat. Once almost cooked, set aside and allow to continue cooking in the pan.

To Serve

Swipe a spoonful of purée across the plate. Place 3 slices of black pudding on top. Carve the venison and place onto the purée. Garnish with the lettuce. Finish by adding a little of the orange and vanilla reduction.

PEANUT MOUSSE WITH SALTED CARAMEL GANACHE & FEUILLETINE

SERVES 8

A refreshing Cornish elderflower pressé from Cornish Orchards (England)

Ingredients

Peanut Mousse

150g crunchy peanut butter
105ml full-fat milk
5 leaves gelatine (softened in cold water)
225g egg whites
150g caster sugar
500ml double cream (lightly whipped)

Salted Caramel Ganache

295g caster sugar
52g butter
50g cocoa butter
575ml double cream
26g glucose
3 gelatine leaves (softened in cold water)
425g 39% milk chocolate
15g Cornish sea salt

Gianduja

175g 55% milk chocolate
80g praline paste

Feuilletine Base

180g 35% dark chocolate
110g gianduja
210g praline paste
35g salted butter
105g hazelnuts (finely chopped)
135g walnuts (chopped)
175g feuilletine wafers

Garnish

tempered chocolate pieces
white chocolate (finely grated)

8 silicone mini loaf moulds
parchment paper

Method

For The Peanut Mousse (Prepare ahead)

Warm the peanut butter and milk together, add the softened gelatine, then set aside to cool.

Whisk the egg whites to soft peak stage, add the caster sugar and whisk for a further 2 minutes. Fold the mixture into the lightly whipped cream, then fold in the peanut mix. Pour into silicone moulds, freeze for 6 hours.

For The Salted Caramel Ganache

Dry caramelise the sugar. When a golden colour is achieved, add the butter and cocoa butter.

Warm the cream and glucose together in a separate pan, then add the caramel mix. Squeeze the gelatine to remove any excess water and add to the pan. Slowly add the chocolate over a very low heat. Season with salt. Blend to *emulsify* and leave in a cool place to set.

For The Gianduja

Melt the chocolate and paste together over a *bain-marie* until smooth. Leave to set.

For The Feuilletine Base

Heat the chocolate and gianduja to 45°C, add the praline and cool to 38°C. Add the butter and mix to *emulsify*. Once mixed, combine with the hazelnuts and walnuts before adding the wafers and mixing until fully incorporated. Pour the mixture onto parchment paper and place another sheet on top. Roll to a thickness of 3mm, then allow to set in a cool place. When set, cut into rectangles 5mm bigger all round than the peanut mousse moulds.

To Serve

Place the feuilletine base on a large plate and add the peanut mousse on top. Pipe the caramel ganache on top of the mousse. Garnish with tempered chocolate and dust with finely grated white chocolate.

Chef's Tip

This can be made in advance. It can also be frozen and served as a parfait.

116
THE ROYAL HOTEL RESTAURANT

The Royal Hotel, Belgrave Road, Ventnor, Isle of Wight, PO38 1JJ

01983 852 186
www.royalhoteliow.co.uk Twitter: @Royalhoteliow

The restaurant at The Royal excels in serving uncomplicated British food that mirrors the seasons, influenced by its enviable location between coast and countryside. The team believe in supporting the many superlative food producers on the Isle of Wight, which not only cuts down food miles but guarantees they are using the freshest, most flavoursome ingredients in the kitchen. Nearby, a family-run farm delivers organic fruit and vegetables, including heirloom varieties and heritage potatoes, as well as modern hybrids. In the summer months, the chefs can pick fresh herbs and berries from the hotel's own kitchen garden, with home-grown strawberries going into the jam for the afternoon tea menu.

Choosing seasonal produce wherever possible ensures that the menu always reflects what is ripe and ready to eat. It also stimulates the creativity of the talented chefs to work within the confines of what is freshly available. A great deal of passion, time and culinary invention goes into preparing the constantly changing menu.

"We believe in supporting the many great food suppliers here on the Isle of Wight, says head chef Steven Harris. "Staying true to our heritage whilst trying new techniques and modern hybrid vegetables from family-run farms is important to us. Dining at The Royal will always be a gastronomic highlight of your stay."

The Royal is one of the finest hotels on the island and shares the rare privilege of being one of only 30 establishments to be listed in every Michelin Guide since it was first published in 1911. The Royal kitchen has held 2 AA Rosettes for excellent food for over 20 years.

VENTNOR BAY CRAB SALAD, BROWN MEAT BAVAROIS, MANGO, PINK GRAPEFRUIT, CRAB TUILE

SERVES 6

 Sancerre, La Vigne Blanche, Domaine Henri Bourgeois (France)

Ingredients

Bavarois

100ml full-fat milk
85ml whipping cream
2g agar agar
100g brown crab meat
1g salt
cayenne pepper (pinch of)

White Crab Meat

300g white crab meat
2 tbsp mayonnaise
1 lemon (juice of)
20g parsley (chopped)

Crab Tuile

100g brown crab meat
10g caster sugar
60g plain flour
200ml cold water
160g butter (melted)

Garnish

1 grapefruit
1 mango
oyster cress

6 rings (12cm diameter)

Method

For The Bavarois

Wrap the rings in cling film to create a mould.

Bring the milk and cream to the boil and whisk in the agar agar.

Put the crab meat into a blender and add the milk and cream mix. Blend for 1 minute at high speed. Season with the salt and cayenne, then pass through a fine sieve and pour into the moulds immediately. Leave to set in the fridge for 10-15 minutes.

For The White Crab Meat

Mix all the ingredients together in a bowl.

For The Crab Tuile (Not pictured)

Combine all the ingredients together in a bowl, gradually whisking in the melted butter.

Cook in batches in a non-stick frying pan until evenly golden brown. Store on a paper lined tray.

For The Garnish

Segment the grapefruit and chop each segment into 3.

Peel and dice the mango into 1cm cubes.

To Serve

Assemble as pictured, topping with the oyster cress and with 5 pieces of mango and grapefruit on each plate.

Chef's Tip

Add pink grapefruit for sharpness; it works beautifully with the sweet crab.

ROASTED DUCK BREAST, RAVIOLO OF LEG, ARTICHOKE, BROCCOLI, PAK CHOI, DUCK JUS

SERVES 6

 Château Le Pey Cru Bourgeois Medoc (France)

Ingredients

3 large duck breasts (skin on)

Artichoke Purée

1½kg Jerusalem artichokes (un-peeled, thoroughly washed, roughly chopped)
oil (to sauté)
water (to cover)
100ml whipping cream
100g butter, salt

Ravioli Filling

3 duck legs, oil (to *confit*)
15g parsley (chopped)
12g ground ginger
35g stem ginger (diced)
sherry vinegar (splash of)
75ml duck sauce, salt (pinch of)

Pasta Dough

300g strong flour
4 medium eggs, 2 egg yolks
2 tbsp olive oil, salt (pinch of)

Duck Jus

1 carrot, 1 stick celery
1 large onion, 1 leek
1 stick lemongrass, 1 head beetroot
3 thin slices ginger, 1 lime leaf
sherry vinegar (splash of)
100ml red wine, 100ml ruby port
2 duck carcases (chopped, roasted)
3 litres brown chicken stock
seasoning
lemon juice (spritz of, to taste)

Garnish

broccoli stalk, pak choi leaf
artichoke crisps

Method

For The Artichoke Purée

Place the artichokes in a large saucepan with a little oil. Cook on a medium heat until golden brown.

Add the water, whipping cream and seasoning and cook slowly until very soft. Strain and place in a blender whilst adding the butter a little at a time. Purée until smooth.

For The Ravioli Filling (Prepare ahead)

Preheat the oven to 120°C.

Place the duck legs in a tray, cover with oil and cook in the oven for 4 hours. Once cooled, pick the meat off the legs. Place into a bowl with the remaining ingredients. Roll into 50g balls.

Chef's Tip

Salt the duck legs for 12 hours to draw out the moisture and tenderise the meat.

For The Pasta Dough

Blend the ingredients together until they form a dough. Rest for 2 hours. Roll out the pasta on a machine to setting 2.

To Form The Ravioli

Cut 12 discs from the pasta. Place a small amount of the ravioli filling in the centre of each disc. Lightly wet round the edges of the pasta and place another disc on top, ensuring that the filling is secured carefully between the pasta discs.

For The Duck Jus

Roughly chop the vegetables and colour in a pan with the ginger and lime leaf. Add the vinegar, port and wine and reduce to a syrup. Stir in the bones and stock, simmer for 1 hour. Pass through a sieve and reduce to a sauce consistency. Season to taste. Pass through a fine sieve. Finish with a squeeze of lemon juice.

For The Garnish

Peel the broccoli stalk and cook in salted water for 4 minutes. *Blanch* the pak choi in salted, boiling water for 1 minute.

To Cook The Duck And Serve

Cook the duck breasts slowly skin-side down for 6 minutes. Turn and cook on the flesh for 5 minutes. Allow to rest.

Cook the ravioli for 4 minutes in salted water. Carefully arrange on the plate with all the other elements as pictured.

RHUBARB CRUMBLE & CUSTARD

SERVES 8

 Peller Estates Riesling Icewine, Niagara Peninsula (Canada)

Ingredients

2½kg rhubarb (juiced)

Custard Cassonade

½ vanilla pod (seeds of)
3 egg yolks
42g sugar
300ml double cream

Rhubarb Jelly

25g sugar
3g agar agar
280ml rhubarb juice
10g gelatine (soaked in cold water)

Rhubarb Liquor

300ml rhubarb juice
100g sugar
2 balls stem ginger (roughly chopped)
10ml grenadine syrup

Rhubarb Gel

300ml rhubarb liquor
25g sugar
5g agar agar

Rhubarb Sorbet

500ml rhubarb juice
275ml water
250g sugar
100g glucose powder

Crumble

100g caster sugar
200g butter
300g plain flour

8 ring moulds (lined with cling film)

Method

For The Custard Cassonade

Preheat the oven to 95°C.

Scrape the vanilla pod and put the seeds in a bowl with the egg yolks and sugar, whisk well.

Heat the cream and pour over the mixture whilst whisking. Pour into lined ring moulds and cook until there is a slight wobble, approximately 40-45 minutes. Best served at room temperature.

For The Rhubarb Jelly

Mix the sugar and agar agar with the juice, bring to the boil and simmer for 2 minutes. Add the gelatine and leave to set in a flat tray. Once the jelly is firm, dice into 1cm cubes..

For The Rhubarb Liquor

Combine the ingredients and bring to the boil. Remove from the heat and allow to cool. Strain.

For The Rhubarb Gel

Place all of the ingredients in a pan, reserving 50ml of the liquor until the end. Bring to the boil. Remove from the heat and allow to cool for about 10 minutes until set. Transfer into a blender and blend on full power until you have a silky, smooth gel, adjusting the consistency with the remaining rhubarb liquor if necessary.

For The Rhubarb Sorbet

Add all the ingredients together and bring to the boil. Allow to cool, then churn in an ice cream machine. Freeze until required.

For The Crumble

Preheat the oven to 180°C.

Cream together the sugar and butter. Add the flour and rub through your fingers to form breadcrumbs.

Bake in the oven for 20-25 minutes until cooked.

To Serve

Spread the rhubarb gel in the centre of the plate and place the custard cassonade on top. Arrange the jelly around the cassonade with the crumble spooned half on, half off the cassonade. Place the sorbet on the crumble to stop it sliding around.

Chef's Tip

Make sure you mix the crumble with a fork every 5 minutes to avoid making shortbread. You will need to juice about 2½kg of rhubarb to make just over 1 litre of juice.

126
SAMPHIRE BISTRO

36 Arweanck Street, Falmouth, Cornwall, TR11 5JE

01326 210 759
www.samphire-falmouth.co.uk Twitter: @samphirefal

nspired by the infamous bistros of Paris, but with a modern, Cornish twist, Samphire Bistro promises beautifully cooked, authentic dishes at affordable prices, and fresh, local, seasonal ingredients whenever possible.

Chef-patron Dave Trewin and his partner Emily opened Samphire in 2010, naming the restaurant after their favourite local ingredient - foraged samphire, which as you might imagine, features on the menu as often as it can! Other Samphire Bistro favourites diners can expect to find on the menu include; French onion soup, lobster, seafood platter, onglet steak and for dessert, Samphire's chocolate delice and crème brûlée.

Located within walking distance of the sea front, a selection of fresh fish is always readily available.

"We have exceptional contacts with the guys on the day boats, who make sure we get the very best fish and shellfish that they catch - it's a privileged position to be in," says Dave.

Samphire's honest approach to clean-tasting, simple food, locally sourced and packed with flavour, has been rewarded with a listing in both the Michelin and Trencherman's guides. Focusing on quality and consistency, every guest dining at Samphire Bistro will feel they've had a great meal in a really welcoming environment.

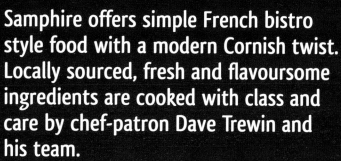

Samphire offers simple French bistro style food with a modern Cornish twist. Locally sourced, fresh and flavoursome ingredients are cooked with class and care by chef-patron Dave Trewin and his team.

BON APPÉTIT

· LE PLAT ·   · LA TASSE ·

LA CUISINE

FALMOUTH BAY SCALLOPS, PEA & BACON RISOTTO, CRISPY KALE

SERVES 4

 Polgoon Madeleine Angevine White, 2014
Cornwall (England)

Ingredients

Pea And Bacon Risotto

200g bacon (diced)
300g frozen baby peas
2 tbsp olive oil
1 small onion (diced)
400g Arborio rice
125ml dry white wine
1½ litres chicken stock (hot)
1 tbsp unsalted butter
50g Parmigiano Reggiano cheese (finely grated)
½ lemon (juice of)
Cornish sea salt (to season)
freshly ground pepper (to season)

Scallops

12 scallops
oil (for frying)
salt and pepper (to season)

Crispy Kale

kale (handful of)

To Serve

lemon juice (spritz of)

Method

For The Pea And Bacon Risotto

Fry the bacon in a pan over a moderate heat until crisp. Drain the bacon on a paper towel and reserve 1 tablespoon of the bacon fat.

Purée half of the peas with 225ml of water in a food processor.

Heat a large saucepan with a little oil, add the onion and cook over a moderate heat for 5 minutes until softened. Pour in the rice and continue to stir until the rice is evenly coated with the oil. Add the wine and simmer until almost evaporated, about 3 minutes.

Add enough chicken stock to just cover the rice and cook over a moderate heat, stirring continuously, until the stock has been absorbed. Add a little more stock to cover the rice. Continue cooking and stirring, and adding more stock as it's absorbed, until the rice is *al dente* and suspended in a creamy sauce. This will take about 25 minutes.

Stir in the pea purée, the remaining peas and bacon and cook, stirring, until hot. Remove the risotto from the heat and stir in the butter, reserved bacon fat, grated Parmesan and lemon juice. Season with salt and pepper.

Chef's Tip

Prepare the risotto ahead and spread thin to chill. You can quickly reheat in a pan to make an impressive starter for dinner guests.

To Cook The Scallops

Dry the scallops on a paper towel.

Heat a thin film of oil in a frying pan until hot. Add the scallops and cook for about 1-1½ minutes on each side until golden. Season with salt and pepper.

For The Crispy Kale

Drop a handful of kale into a deep fat fryer for 30 seconds to crisp. Remove and place onto a paper towel until ready to plate.

To Assemble

Spoon 3 mounds of risotto onto each plate and top each with a scallop. Arrange the crispy kale on top and finish with a squeeze of lemon juice over each scallop.

TRIO OF CORNISH FISH, CHORIZO, TOMATO & BUTTERBEAN STEW, POTATO GRIDDLE CAKE

SERVES 4

 Camel Valley Bacchus, 2013
(England)

Ingredients

Tomato And Butterbean Stew

200g chorizo (diced)
½ tbsp olive oil or rapeseed oil
1 red onion (finely chopped)
2 cloves garlic (chopped)
2 sprigs rosemary (leaves picked)
400g tin butterbeans (drained)
1kg tomatoes (cut into 8, cores removed)
300ml chicken stock
200g spinach
2 tbsp flat leaf parsley (chopped)
seasoning

Potato Griddle Cakes

250g mashed potatoes
1 tsp baking powder
100g plain flour
salt and freshly ground black pepper
1 tbsp fresh thyme
2 tbsp vegetable oil

Fish

2 monkfish tails (filleted, trimmed, halved)
2 small haddock (filleted, scaled, pin boned)
2 sole (filleted, split down the middle)
salt and pepper
oil (for frying)

To Serve

200g French beans (trimmed)
1 tbsp butter
200g spring greens (sliced)
lemon (spritz of)
parsley (chopped)

Method

For The Tomato And Butterbean Stew

Fry the chorizo in olive oil over a medium heat in a large pan for 2-3 minutes. Add the onion and cook for 10 minutes, adding the garlic and rosemary for the final 2 minutes.

Stir in the butterbeans, tomatoes and stock. Bring to a gentle simmer, then cover and cook for 10 minutes until thickened. Stir in the spinach and parsley until the spinach is just wilted. Season to taste.

For The Potato Griddle Cakes

Mix all the ingredients together in a bowl until well combined, then shape the potato mixture into 8 patties. Heat the oil in a frying pan and fry the patties for 3-4 minutes on each side, or until crisp and golden brown on both sides.

To Cook The Fish

Heat 3 frying pans with a little oil. Season the fish with salt and pepper. Place the 4 pieces of monkfish into the first pan, followed by the haddock skin-side down into the second, and cook for about 3-4 minutes. Turn over the monkfish, now add the sole skin-side down in the third pan and cook for a further 3-5 minutes. Turn over the sole and haddock, then remove all 3 pans from heat.

Chef's Tip

Buy your fish from a good fishmonger - he will do the preparation for you.

To Serve

Cook the French beans in a pan with a little water and butter for 3 minutes, adding the spring greens halfway through. Arrange the stew, vegetables and potato cakes onto the plates. Stack the fish on top and finish with a squeeze of lemon and a sprinkle of parsley.

APPLE TART TATIN WITH TOASTED ALMOND ICE CREAM

SERVES 4

 Quady, Elysium Black Muscat
California (USA)

Ingredients

Toasted Almond Ice Cream

300ml full-fat milk
300ml double cream
200g flaked almonds (toasted)
6 egg yolks
150g caster sugar

Apple Tart Tatin

200g puff pastry
100g Demerara sugar
4 large apples (cored, cut into wedges)
40g unsalted butter

To Garnish

flaked almonds (toasted)

Method

For The Toasted Almond Ice Cream (Prepare ahead)

Warm the milk, cream and almonds in a heavy-bottomed saucepan over a medium heat until a few bubbles appear along the edge of the pan. Remove from the heat and infuse for at least 15 minutes. Pour through a fine mesh sieve into a jug.

Whisk together the egg yolks and sugar in a bowl until light and fluffy, about 3-4 minutes. While whisking, pour the milk mixture into the egg yolk mixture.

Return the mixture to the pan, set over a medium-low heat and cook, stirring continuously until the custard thickens slightly, about 5 minutes. Do not let the custard boil. Pour the mixture into a bowl and allow to cool. Cover and refrigerate until very cold. Churn in an ice cream machine. Freeze until firm, at least 2 hours.

For The Apple Tart Tatin

On a lightly floured surface, roll out the puff pastry to 2mm thick. Prick it all over with a fork and transfer to a baking tray. Cover with cling film and refrigerate for 20-30 minutes to prevent shrinkage while cooking.

Cut the pastry into 4 circles (10cm diameter) using a plate as a template. Prick with a fork and chill.

Preheat the oven to 190°C.

Divide the sugar between 4 small pans (12cm) and heat over a medium heat until the sugar dissolves. Arrange the apples in a fan shape around the bottom of each pan. Scatter the butter around and leave until a golden caramel has formed. Place a pastry lid on top of the apples and transfer to the oven for 15-20 minutes until the pastry is golden and crisp. Put back on the hob and warm a little to help turn the tart out.

To Serve

Place a large dinner plate over the tart and, holding the pan and plate together, turn it upside down, shaking it sideways gently to release the tart onto the plate.

Serve with a scoop of ice cream and some toasted almonds as pictured.

Chef's Tip

This tart can be made as one larger tart and also is amazing with Cornish clotted cream.

136
SAUNTON SANDS HOTEL

Saunton, Braunton, North Devon, EX33 1LQ

01271 890 212
www.sauntonsands.co.uk Twitter: @SauntonSandsHot Facebook: Saunton Sands Hotel

With possibly the most stunning views in the South West, lunch or dinner at Saunton Sands Hotel's smartly refurbished art deco restaurant on the North Devon Coast is an experience to savour.

Head chef Jamie Colman, a quarter finalist on BBC Masterchef: The Professionals, creates seasonal, modern cuisine that has gained the hotel an AA Rosette as well as inclusion in the prestigious Trencherman's Guide.

In 2015 Jamie returned to his home in North Devon to join the hotel in his first head chef post. This position follows a career that has included working for Gordon Ramsay at his Michelin starred restaurant in Claridge's and for Michael Caines at 2 Michelin starred Gidleigh Park. He also came second in the San Pellegrino Young Chef of the Year (UK and Ireland).

Guests can enjoy a smart supper with wines that have been carefully chosen by Susy Atkins (BBC Saturday Kitchen and Sunday Telegraph's Stella Magazine's wine expert), a luxurious classic afternoon tea in the Terrace Lounge, or a gourmet burger at the hotel's shorefront café, The Beachside Grill, serving an authentic grill menu.

Saunton Hotel prides itself on good food and providing an unforgettable experience. With the recent refurbishment of the hotel's Gallery (bar and lounge), alongside many of the rooms and apartments, it's undeniable that the high standard of cooking is now echoed in the hotel's divine décor and smart service.

Quality service and wonderful experiences are the main focus of this family-run hotel. With a breathtaking view of one of Britain's best beaches, drawing in surfers, walkers and extreme sports enthusiasts, this well-loved establishment is truly a special place.

SURF AND SEA VIEWS ←

SMOKED CREEDY CARVER DUCK BREAST, BEETROOT, PICKLED WALNUT, BUCKWHEAT BRIOCHE

SERVES 4

 Rongopai Pinot Noir
(New Zealand)

Ingredients

Smoked Duck

1 whole Creedy Carver duck (including giblets)
60g salt, 60g sugar
5g five-spice
1 orange (zest of)

Duck Parfait

25ml port, 25ml Madeira
25ml brandy
1 clove garlic (finely chopped)
1 shallot (chopped)
50g duck liver
50g butter

Buckwheat Brioche (Makes 6-8)

4 large eggs
3 tbsp full-fat milk
50g buckwheat flour
20g rice flour, 50g butter
30g sugar, 3g salt

Pickled Walnut Purée

1 shallot (chopped), 1 clove garlic (chopped)
2 sprigs tarragon (picked)
1 jar pickled walnuts

Beetroot

100g yellow beetroot (peeled, diced)
100g candy beetroot (peeled)
½ tsp ginger (freshly grated)
olive oil (drizzle of)

Garnish

8g beetroot powder, nasturtium leaves

oak chippings (to smoke)
6-8 paper cups

Method

For The Smoked Duck Breast (Prepare ahead)

Remove the duck breasts from the bone. Combine all the other ingredients, rub over the duck flesh and leave for 8 hours in the fridge. Wash off the salt mix and pat the breasts dry. Smoke over the oak chippings for 5 minutes. Seal the breasts in a hot pan, then cook in a water bath (60°C) for 45 minutes.

Alternatively, after sealing the breasts, cook in the oven (180°C fan) for 8 minutes. Leave to rest until ready to plate.

For The Duck Parfait

Reduce the port, Madeira and brandy with the garlic and shallot until it forms a syrup. Place the duck liver into a blender with the butter and syrup. Blitz until smooth, then cook in a *bain-marie* at 110°C for 50 minutes. When cool, beat until smooth, then transfer to a piping bag.

For The Buckwheat Brioche

Mix all of the ingredients in a blender until smooth. Pour the mixture into an espuma gun and charge with 3 chargers. Make a small hole in the bottom of each paper cup. Fill halfway with the brioche mix. Microwave on full power for 1 minute.

If you don't have an espuma gun, add 1 teaspoon of baking powder to the mix and cook in the same way.

For The Pickled Walnut Purée

Sauté the shallots, garlic and tarragon until softened. Add the walnuts, then cover with water. Cook gently for about 10 minutes, then blitz until smooth.

For The Beetroot

Cook the yellow beetroot in seasoned water until tender. Mix the ginger with the olive oil. Finely slice the candy beetroot and drizzle with the seasoned oil.

To Assemble The Dish

Swipe the walnut purée on the plate and place the duck pieces as desired. Dot with parfait and arrange the beetroot and brioche. To finish, dust with the beetroot powder and garnish with nasturtium leaves.

Chef's Tip

Wrap the beetroot powder in muslin cloth to enable easy dusting of the plate.

POOLE BATTEN FARM PORK, BRIXHAM SCALLOP, SAVOY CABBAGE, PARSNIP, SMOKED BACON JUS

SERVES 4

 *Puligny-Montrachet
(France)*

Ingredients

Pork And Scallops

200g salt
200g sugar
800g pork belly
500g duck fat
2 pork chops
4 scallops

Smoked Bacon Jus

1 onion (sliced)
1 clove garlic (crushed)
oil (to sauté)
10 rashers smoked bacon
1 sprig thyme
200ml chicken stock
200ml veal jus
5ml double cream

Parsnip Purée

500g parsnips (roughly chopped)
500ml full-fat milk
salt (to season)

Garnish

3 large parsnips
1 Savoy cabbage
butter (knob of)

Method

For The Pork And Scallops (Prepare the day before)

Mix the salt and sugar together, rub over the pork belly and cure for 6 hours.

Preheat the oven to 100°C (fan).

Wash the cure off the belly, then cover in the duck fat. Cook for 10 hours.

Remove from the oven and press under a heavy tray overnight. Cut into portions.

Cook the pork chops *sous vide* (58°C) for 1 hour, then refresh. Alternatively, seal the chops in a hot pan and cook in the oven (180°C fan) for 14 minutes. Rest for 5 minutes.

Clean the scallops and set aside.

> **Chef's Tip**
>
> Use a good quality, high fat content English pork to achieve the best possible flavour.

For The Smoked Bacon Jus

Sauté the onion and garlic in a little oil until coloured. Add the smoked bacon, allowing it to crisp up before adding the thyme and chicken stock. Reduce by half, add the veal jus and reduce by a quarter. Pass through a fine sieve and finish with a dash of cream.

For The Parsnip Purée

Bring the parsnips to the boil with the milk and salt. When cooked, blitz until smooth.

For The Garnish

Using a sharp knife, cut 2 of the parsnips into 8 cone shapes. Finely slice the remaining parsnip into strips using a mandolin. Deep fry (160°C) the strips until crisp. Cut the Savoy cabbage into the desired shape.

To Assemble The Dish

Preheat the oven to 180°C (fan).

Crisp the pork belly and pork chop in a hot pan, place into the oven for 6 minutes to warm through. Roast the parsnips in foaming butter until golden. *Blanch* the cabbage in seasoned, boiling water, drain, then char with a blow torch. Cook the scallops in a hot pan and leave to rest for 2 minutes. Carve the pork chop in half and plate with a swipe of parsnip purée, parsnip cones and Savoy pieces. Garnish with parsnip crisps and the jus.

PISTACHIO & RAPESEED OIL CAKE, RHUBARB SORBET

SERVES 8

 Freixenet Cordon Rosado
(Spain)

Ingredients

Pistachio And Rapeseed Oil Sponge

3 medium eggs
200g caster sugar
125ml rapeseed oil
100g butter (melted)
220g pistachios
50g polenta
75g plain flour
1 tsp baking powder
2 oranges (zest and juice of)
2 lemons (zest and juice of)

Rhubarb Sorbet

490ml water
125g glucose
20g inverted sugar
375g caster sugar
9g procrema
1kg rhubarb purée

Poached Rhubarb

450g rhubarb
375ml port
375ml red wine
350g caster sugar

Rhubarb Gel

250g rhubarb (chopped)
100ml lemon juice
100g caster sugar

Garnish

rhubarb sherbet
candied pistachios

12cm square cake tin

Method

For The Pistachio And Rapeseed Oil Sponge

Preheat the oven to 150°C (fan).

Whisk the eggs and sugar together to firm peaks. Slowly add the oil and butter.

Blitz the dry ingredients with the citrus zest and juice, then fold into the wet mix. Bake for 25 minutes.

For The Rhubarb Sorbet

Bring the water, glucose, inverted sugar, sugar and procrema to the boil in a pan. Whisk in the rhubarb purée and leave to cool. Churn in an ice cream machine.

Chef's Tip

The key to great sorbet is to get the correct balance of sugar and fats for the perfect smoothness.

For The Poached Rhubarb

Chop the rhubarb into batons. Bring the port, red wine and sugar to the boil, add the rhubarb and cook for 1 minute. Leave to cool in the liquid.

For The Rhubarb Gel

Cook the chopped rhubarb in the lemon and sugar mixture until tender. Blitz until smooth.

To Assemble The Dish

Portion the sponge into finger-size pieces and place on the plate. Place the poached rhubarb as pictured and dust with sherbet. Add dots of rhubarb gel. Finish with a scoop of sorbet. Garnish with candied pistachios.

146
SPINNAKERS
RESTAURANT

The Fowey Hotel, Esplanade, Fowey, Cornwall, PL23 1HX

01726 832 551 (option 0)
www.thefoweyhotel.co.uk Twitter: @thefoweyhotel

Tucked away in the South West corner of the Fowey Hotel, in the beautiful Cornish village by the same name, you will find the 2 AA Rosette award-winning Spinnakers Restaurant. Spinnakers is a light and airy room, with ornate high ceilings and soft pastel tones, a design that works in perfect harmony with the Victorian architecture of the iconic building that hosts it. The restaurant offers its diners an easy ambience, exceptional service, unrivalled panoramic views of the Fowey Estuary and the very best of Cornish cuisine.

The kitchen is under direction from head chef Mark Griffiths. Mark and his team are renowned for taking pride in the local ingredients that can be found right on the doorstep of the hotel grounds, from the fresh fish in the estuary to the livestock reared in the acres of rolling green Cornish farmlands. The team works to create expertly balanced, complex, yet traditional dishes with a strong emphasis on flavour and texture.

Spinnakers works to an ethos of simple, fresh, sustainable, local and seasonal and as such, whether you are just popping in for a snack in the bar, or a three-course fine dining experience, Spinnakers is one of the best places in Cornwall to excite the senses.

Spinnakers Restaurant, with 2 AA Rosettes, focuses on quality ingredients, locally sourced and beautifully presented food. The restaurant offers its diners an easy ambience, exceptional service and unrivalled panoramic views of the Fowey Estuary.

PRESSED BELLY OF PORK

SERVES 4

 Knightor Pinot Gris 2011
Cornwall (England)

Ingredients

Pressed Belly Of Pork

400g pork belly
1 leek (chopped)
1 carrot (chopped)
1 onion (chopped)
2 cloves garlic (chopped)
300ml vegetable stock
300ml apple juice
1 tbsp oil
salt (sprinkle of)

Beetroot Base

1 large beetroot

Apple Purée

1 cooking apple (peeled, cored, sliced)
20g caster sugar
20ml water

Remoulade

20g celeriac (finely grated)
1 Braeburn apple (finely grated)
15g parsley (chopped)
½ tsp coarse grain mustard
15g mayonnaise
seasoning (to taste)

Red Onion Marmalade Wonton

100g red onion
25g redcurrant jelly
125ml red wine
125ml orange juice
4 wonton pastry sheets
1 egg (beaten)

Garnish

crackling

Method

For The Belly Of Pork (Prepare ahead)
Preheat the oven to 170°C.
Place the belly into an ovenproof dish with the leek, carrot, onion, garlic, stock and apple juice. Cover and braise in the oven for 3 hours.
Remove the belly pork from the liquor and place between 2 trays. Apply a weight to press and leave to cool. When cool, wrap the pressed belly pork in cling film and refrigerate until ready to assemble.
Preheat the oven to 190°C.
Thinly slice the pork skin and place in a bowl with the oil and a sprinkle of salt and mix. Place on a rack and cook for 15-20 minutes until crisp.

For The Beetroot Base
Cover the beetroot with water and simmer until tender, approximately 4 minutes. Remove from the heat and allow to cool. Thinly slice the beetroot as a base for your belly pork. Refrigerate until ready to serve.

For The Apple Purée
Cook the apple slices with the sugar and water until tender. Drain, then blend to a smooth purée.

For The Remoulade
Carefully combine all the ingredients, season to taste and refrigerate until required.

For The Red Onion Marmalade Wonton
Combine the red onions with the redcurrant jelly, orange juice and red wine in a pan. Place on a low heat and stir occasionally until a jam consistency is formed. Remove from the heat and leave to cool.
Lay the wonton pastry sheets flat and egg wash the edges. Fill with the red onion marmalade and pinch together.

To Assemble
Remove the belly pork from the fridge and trim into 4 portions. Gently pan fry until golden on all sides. Place in the oven at 180°C. until hot.
Deep fry (180°C) the wonton pastry until golden.
Lay the beetroot slices as a base in the centre of each plate. Place the belly pork on top. Garnish with the apple purée, remoulade and crackling.

Chef's Tip
If your pork is cooked but the crackling is not quite crisp enough, just remove the crackling by slicing it away as close to the meat as possible. Put it back in the oven or under a grill to crisp up while the rest of the meat rests.

FILLET OF STONE BASS

SERVES 4

 Château Le Coin Sauvignon Gris 2014, Bordeaux (France)

Ingredients

Stone Bass And Vine Tomatoes

4 x 160g stone bass fillets
200g vine tomatoes

Butternut Squash Purée

150g butternut squash (diced)
20g shallots
2 cloves garlic

Sauce Vierge

100ml extra virgin olive oil
100g plum tomatoes (diced)
20g shallots (diced)
10g capers
½ lemon (juice of)
parsley (chopped, pinch of)
seasoning (to taste)

Vegetables

8 Cornish new potatoes (washed)
saffron strands (pinch of)
100g mixed peppers (sliced)
200ml extra virgin oil
200g bok choy
50g butter
50ml water

Method

For The Stone Bass And Vine Tomatoes

Preheat the oven to 200°C.

Cook the stone bass skin-side down in a hot, non-stick pan until the skin is crisp and golden. Turn the fillets and seal the flesh, then place in the oven with the vine tomatoes for approximately 4 minutes (depending on size of fillets).

Chef's Tip

If you want to prepare in advance, cook the fillets of fish on the skin-side only and then set aside on a baking tray.
They can then be cooked for just 4 minutes in a hot oven just before you are ready to eat.

For The Butternut Squash Purée

Steam the butternut squash, shallots and garlic until soft. Blend to a smooth purée.

For The Sauce Vierge

Combine all the ingredients in a bowl and mix well. Season to taste.

For The Vegetables

Place the potatoes in cold water with the saffron. Leave to infuse for 1 hour. Bring to the boil and simmer until cooked.

Immerse the peppers into the extra virgin oil and gently simmer until soft. Drain.

Place the bok choy, butter and water in a pan and stir on medium heat until wilted. Season and drain.

To Assemble

Serve the stone bass on a bed of bok choy and accompany with potatoes and vine tomatoes. Add a swipe of warm butternut squash purée and a little sauce vierge. To finish, garnish with the *confit* peppers.

TEXTURES OF LEMON AND RHUBARB

SERVES 8

 Les Charmes de Bastor Lamontagne 2008 France)

Ingredients

Pastry Cases

180g white flour
60g icing sugar
80g butter
salt (pinch of)
1 egg

Raspberry Coulis

250g raspberries
20g icing sugar
½ lemon (juice of)

Rhubarb

200g rhubarb (prepped)
200ml orange juice
40g caster sugar
½ stick cinnamon
½ star anise

Lemon Curd

135g caster sugar
135g egg (beaten, approximately 3 eggs)
135ml lemon (juice of)
175g butter
1½ leaves gelatine (soaked in cold water)

Lemon Mousse

1 leaf gelatine (soaked in cold water)
200ml double cream
90g natural yoghurt
½ lemon (juice and zest of)
45g icing sugar

Meringue

80g egg white (approximately 3 eggs)
160g caster sugar

Garnish

seasonal berries

8 mini tart cases

Method

To Make The Pastry Cases (Prepare ahead)
Combine the flour, icing sugar, butter and salt, then stir in the egg. Wrap in cling film and refrigerate for 1 hour.
Divide the pastry into 8 equal amounts and roll to 3-4mm thick and line the tart cases. Freeze for 20 minutes.
Preheat the oven to 170°C.
Blind bake the cases for 12 minutes, remove the beans and place back in the oven for 2 minutes until lightly golden.

> **Chef's Tip**
> The pastry cases can be made up to 2 days ahead.
> They freeze well.

For The Raspberry Coulis
Gently cook the raspberries, icing sugar and lemon juice over a low heat until the raspberries have broken down. Blend to a purée, pass through a fine sieve and chill.

For The Rhubarb
Preheat the oven to 180°C.
Braise the rhubarb with the orange juice, sugar, cinnamon and star anise in an oven tray for 10 minutes until tender. Leave to cool. Refrigerate until required.

For The Lemon Curd
Mix the sugar, egg and lemon juice together in a pan and slowly bring to the boil whilst continuously stirring. Once it reaches the boil, remove from the heat and whisk in the butter and gelatine. Leave to cool.

For The Lemon Mousse
Place the softened gelatine in a pan with 20ml of double cream and dissolve on a low heat.
Mix together the yoghurt, lemon juice, zest and icing sugar into a bowl.
Whip the remaining double cream until soft peaks form.
Stir the gelatine into the yoghurt and lemon mix. Fold in the whipped cream and refrigerate until set, for approximately 2-2½ hours.

For The Meringue
Whisk the egg whites in a bowl until they form soft peaks. Add in the sugar until glossy. Transfer to a piping bag and set aside.

To Assemble
Preheat the oven to 190°C.
Fill the pastry cases with lemon curd and top with the meringue. Bake for 6 minutes, then allow to cool before serving.
Drain the rhubarb and arrange beside the tart. Add the lemon mousse and a swipe of raspberry coulis.
Garnish with seasonal berries.

156
STON EASTON PARK
THE SORREL RESTAURANT

Ston Easton Park, Ston Easton, Near Bath, BA3 4DF

01761 241 631
www.stoneaston.co.uk Twitter: @Stoneaston_park

Nestled in 36 acres of beautiful West Country parkland, Ston Easton Park is unique; this country house hotel is adorned with original antique furniture, sumptuous fabrics and glistening chandeliers, yet the warm welcome and homely atmosphere prevails.

The Sorrel Restaurant at Ston Easton Park, open every day to non-residents and hotel guests, is regarded as one of the best restaurants in Bath, attracting diners from far and wide for special occasions, family celebrations and gourmet dining experiences.

As well as the exquisite Georgian oak-panelled Sorrel Restaurant with spectacular views over the Humphrey Repton landscaped gardens, there are a number of private dining rooms available for intimate celebrations as well as larger dinner parties.

Head chef Martin Baker, who has previously worked with both Gordon Ramsay and Marco Pierre White, creates daily dishes in accordance with the ingredients grown in the hotel's Victorian kitchen garden by dedicated gardeners - Steve and Dale. The dishes are dictated largely on the ingredients available seasonally, producing the best possible flavours.

To complement the award-winning cuisine, the hotel's cellars are famed for their selection of fine wines, vintages and extensive range of New World and table wines.

Not only does the hotel provide a fine dining experience, you can also pay a visit to Ston Easton Park for a quintessentially English afternoon tea, a beautifully British way to spend a leisurely afternoon with friends and family.

Head chef Martin and his dedicated team have enabled The Sorrel Restaurant to maintain its many accolades including 2 AA Rosettes, Silver for Best Hotel Restaurant at the South West Tourism Awards 2014/2015 and Gold for the Taste of the West Awards 2016.

GOAT'S CHEESE PANNA COTTA

MAKES 12 INDIVIDUAL RAMEKINS OR 1 LOAF TIN

 Sauvignon Blanc, Sherwood Stoney Range, Marlborough 2014 (New Zealand)

Ingredients

Goat's Cheese Panna Cotta

1kg goat's cheese (rind removed)
1 litre double cream
½ handful basil
6 cloves garlic
8 leaves gelatine (soaked in water)

Parmesan Circles

500g Parmesan (grated)
1 tbsp poppy seeds

Garnish

2 pink grapefruits (segmented)
1 punnet baby basil
2 radishes (sliced)
2 pomegranates (seeds of)
balsamic syrup (to drizzle)

12 ramekins or 1 loaf tin

Method

For The Goat's Cheese Panna Cotta

Place the goat's cheese in a heatproof bowl with the double cream, basil and garlic cloves. Place the bowl over a pan of simmering water until the cheese has melted. Stir in the gelatine, then pour the mixture through a sieve before pouring into your chosen mould. Leave the mixture to set in the fridge for 2 hours before serving.

Chef's Tip

Your panna cotta should always have a slight wobble.

For The Parmesan Circles

Preheat the oven to 175°C (fan).

Cover a baking tray with baking parchment and sprinkle the grated Parmesan onto the tray. Shape to form circles, then sprinkle the poppy seeds over. Bake for 8-10 minutes until they are a light golden brown.

To Serve

Turn the panna cottas onto the plates. Garnish with the Parmesan circles, grapefruit segments, basil leaves, radishes, pomegranate seeds and a drizzle of balsamic syrup.

LAMB RUMP, LAMB CROQUETTE, WILD GARLIC PUREE, ARTICHOKE PUREE

SERVES 4

 Château Sigognac, Médoc 2010 (France)

Ingredients

2 x 180g lamb rumps

Lamb Croquettes

1 lamb shank
oil (for frying)
1 tbsp paprika
2 shallots (chopped)
2 eggs
2 tbsp flour
4 tbsp breadcrumbs

Lamb Jus

1kg veal, beef, lamb or chicken bones
1 carrot (roughly chopped)
1 leek (roughly chopped)
2 sticks celery (roughly chopped)
1 onion (roughly chopped)
2 sprigs thyme
1 sprig rosemary
2 sprigs curly parsley
2 juniper berries, 1 star anise
water (to cover)
200ml red wine
seasoning

Wild Garlic Purée

1kg wild garlic
500g spinach
285ml double cream

Artichoke Purée

500g Jerusalem artichokes (peeled)
285ml double cream

To Serve

new potatoes
parsley (chopped, sprinkling of)
butter (knob of)
baby carrots
broccoli florets

Method

For The Lamb Croquettes (Prepare ahead)

Preheat the oven to 120°C (fan).

Seal the lamb shank in a frying pan with hot oil. Roll in paprika and braise in the oven for 6-8 hours. Leave to cool, then shred the meat into strands. Add the shallots and 1 egg and mix well. Shape into barrels, *pane* and deep fry (175°C) until crisp.

Chef's Tip

Always cook your lamb pink for maximum flavour.

For The Lamb Jus (Prepare at least 24 hours in advance)

Add all the ingredients, except the red wine, to a large stock pot, cover and simmer for 24 hours. Pass the stock through a fine sieve and reduce down to 500ml.

When the time comes to serve the jus, add the red wine and reduce down further until the jus coats the back of a spoon.

For The Wild Garlic Purée

Blanch the wild garlic and spinach in a pan of boiling water for 10 seconds. Drain the water and place the leaves in a liquidiser with the double cream. Blitz until smooth and a vibrant green. Gently reheat to serve.

For The Artichoke Purée

Boil the artichokes until tender, then add to a liquidiser with the double cream and blitz until smooth. Gently reheat to serve.

To Cook The Lamb Rumps

Preheat the oven to 180°C (fan).

Seal the lamb rumps in a frying pan until the fat is rendered, then place in the oven for 7 minutes. Rest for 10 minutes before serving.

To Serve

Boil the potatoes until soft, drain, then crush. Finish the potatoes by pan frying, then tossing in butter and parsley. Warm the wild garlic and artichoke purées, then plate the dish as pictured, finishing with the lamb jus. Serve with baby carrots and broccoli.

CARAMEL TART WITH LEMON YOGHURT SORBET, CHOCOLATE SOIL & TOFFEE CINDER

SERVES 12

🍷 *Château Roumieu, Sauternes 2012
(France)*

Ingredients

Sweet Pastry

225g plain flour
50g caster sugar
salt (pinch of)
125g butter (diced)
2 medium eggs

Caramel Filling

900ml double cream
540g caster sugar
150g egg yolks (6-8 egg yolks)

Lemon Yoghurt Sorbet

700g sugar
17½g glucose
140g plain yoghurt
75ml lemon juice
57ml water

Chocolate Soil

200g sugar
50ml water
40g white chocolate
40g dark chocolate
40g milk chocolate
20g cocoa
10g ground almonds

Toffee Cinder

125g sugar
50g golden syrup
5g bicarbonate of soda

25cm loose-bottomed tart tin (lightly greased)

Method

For The Sweet Pastry

Combine the flour, sugar and salt in a bowl. Rub in the butter using your fingertips until it resembles breadcrumbs. Bind together gently with the eggs to form a ball. Wrap in cling film and rest in the fridge for 30 minutes.

Preheat the oven to 165°C (fan).

Roll the pastry to ½cm thick on a flour dusted worktop. Carefully line the tin with the pastry, ensuring the pastry is pushed into the sides. Blind bake for 30 minutes until golden brown and trim off the excess pastry once baked.

For The Caramel Filling

Preheat the oven to 130°C (fan).

Heat the cream in a saucepan until boiling.

Heat the sugar in a separate pan over a moderate heat to form a dry caramel. The sugar will start to turn liquid around the edges. When it starts to brown at the edges, drag the sugar towards the centre to prevent any burnt spots. Do not over stir. When a caramel, slowly pour the cream in and whisk until cool. Stir in the egg yolks, then pass the mixture through a sieve to remove any air bubbles. Pour into the pastry case and bake for 30 minutes until the caramel is firm with a slight wobble. Serve at room temperature.

For The Lemon Yoghurt Sorbet

Warm all ingredients together over a low heat and leave to chill in a flat tray. Once chilled, churn in an ice cream machine.

For The Chocolate Soil

Boil the sugar and water in a pan. Add the remaining ingredients, remove from the heat and stir quickly.

For The Toffee Cinder

Line a tray with baking parchment or silicone paper. Heat the sugar and syrup to 150°C. Whisk in the bicarbonate of soda fast and hard then quickly pour onto the lined tray. Store in the freezer until set. Break into shards, then store in an airtight container.

To Serve

Assemble as pictured.

> **Chef's Tip**
>
> Be careful not to burn your caramel as this will leave you with a bitter tasting tart. Also, keep your pastry thin.

166
TALLAND BAY HOTEL

Porthallow, Looe, Cornwall, PL13 2JB

01503 272 667
www.tallandbayhotel.co.uk Twitter: @tallandbayhotel

Talland Bay Hotel is a charming hotel set 150 feet above sea level, with far reaching views out to sea on the idyllic South Cornwall coast, in a quiet rural location on the coastal path between the bustling seafaring towns of Looe and Polperro.

Talland Bay is steeped in history, dating back to the Dooms Day book in 1089. The present house dates back to the 16th Century; until 1919 it was owned by the Trelawnys, an old Cornish family most famous for Bishop Trelawny who was imprisoned in the Tower of London. Porthallow Old House, as it was formerly called, became a hotel in the late 1940s.

Entertaining guests from around the world, Talland Bay Hotel has a warm, welcoming feel with top quality food, extensive drinks and spacious accommodation. 23 rooms give a country house feel, with relaxed, attentive and friendly service.

Dining at Talland Bay is something not to be missed. With the guidance of their imaginative head chef Nick Hawke, the team source only the finest local and seasonal produce, creating stylish menus both in the 2 AA Rosette dining menu or the more relaxed Brasserie menu.

The menus showcase the region, from local farmers to traditional Cornish fishermen. Enjoy dining by warm open log fires in the winter months and al fresco on the terrace, with beautiful sea views, in the summer.

Head chef Nick Hawke has learned his trade under Michelin starred chefs. With his team behind him, he strives to create imaginative, elegant dishes showcasing local produce.

ROASTED CORNISH SCALLOPS, SMOKED ROE TARAMASALATA, CELERIAC, PICKLED APPLE, FOCACCIA WAFER

SERVES 4

 Marco Bonfante Gavi di Gavi
(Italy)

Ingredients

Scallops

12 medium Cornish scallops (seasoned)
butter (knob of), lemon juice (squeeze of)

Smoked Roe Taramasalata

100g smoked cod roe
1 lemon (juice and zest of)
1 clove garlic, 1 tsp smoked paprika
100ml extra virgin olive oil
100ml rapeseed oil

Celeriac Purée

1 medium banana shallot (finely diced)
2 cloves garlic (finely chopped)
1 tsp thyme (chopped)
1 medium celeriac (peeled, diced)
300ml full-fat milk, 50ml cream
salt and pepper (to taste)

Roasted Celeriac

1 small celeriac (cut into 6 equal wedges)
1½ litres vegetable *nage*
1 bulb garlic, 2 sprigs rosemary
1 tbsp whole black peppercorns
2 bay leaves, sea salt

Pickled Apple

2 Granny Smith apples
100ml white wine, 100ml white wine vinegar
100g sugar, 1 sprig dill

Focaccia Wafer

1 small loaf focaccia
extra virgin olive oil (drizzle of)
sea salt (to sprinkle)

Garnish

coriander cress

Method

For The Smoked Roe Taramasalata

Blend the smoked cod roe, lemon juice and zest, garlic and smoked paprika together. Once smooth, slowly add the oil. When incorporated, pass the mix through a fine sieve. Season to taste.

For The Celeriac Purée

Sweat the shallot, garlic and thyme on a medium low heat until the shallots turn translucent. Add the celeriac and sweat for a couple of minutes before adding the milk. Simmer until the celeriac is soft to touch, add the cream, simmer for a couple of minutes, then blend. Pass through a fine sieve and season.

For The Roasted Celeriac

Bring the *nage* to a simmer with the garlic, rosemary, peppercorns and bay leaves. Add the celeriac and cover with a *cartouche*. Simmer for 10 minutes, leave the celeriac to cool in the *nage*. Once cool, remove the celeriac and pan fry until golden brown.

For The Pickled Apple (Prepare ahead)

Make the *gastrique* by bringing the white wine, white wine vinegar and sugar to the boil. Add the dill and leave to cool. Peel and finely dice the apple before adding to the *gastrique*. Refrigerate overnight.

For The Focaccia Wafer (Freeze ahead)

Freeze the focaccia before cutting into fine slices.

Preheat the oven to 120°C (fan).

Drizzle the focaccia slices with olive oil and sprinkle with sea salt. Bake for 30 minutes until crisp.

To Serve

Cut the warm celeriac wedges into thin slices.

Heat a little oil in a frying pan. When it starts to smoke, add the scallops, cook until golden brown, turn and leave for 30 seconds. Finish with a little butter and a squeeze of lemon juice.

Set the scallops to the side of the roasted celeriac. Dot the purée on the plate. Garnish with the pickled apple and coriander cress.

Chef's Tip

Don't season your scallops too early as it will draw out the moisture. You will end up poaching them instead of roasting them in the pan.

CORNISH PORK PLATE

SERVES 4

 Josef Chromy Pinot Noir
(Tasmania)

Ingredients

Confit Pork Belly

5 cloves garlic, 100ml olive oil
smoked Cornish sea salt
1kg pork belly (rind on), 2kg duck fat

Cider Glazed Pork Cheek And Jowl

1 large onion (roughly chopped)
2 large carrots (roughly chopped)
2 sticks celery (roughly chopped)
2 large pig cheeks (including jowl)
1½ litres Cornish mulled cider
1 tsp peppercorns, 2 bay leaves, 2 sprigs sage

Hog's And Black Pudding Terrine

200g unsalted butter
3 cloves garlic, 2 sprigs rosemary
20ml white truffle oil
6 large Maris Piper potatoes (peeled)
500g hog's pudding (thinly sliced)
500g black pudding (thinly sliced)
salt and pepper

Salt Baked Heritage Carrots

250g plain flour, 50g sea salt
1 tbsp rosemary (finely chopped), 100ml water
2 large purple or yellow heritage carrots

Carrot And Star Anise Purée

2 large banana shallots (finely diced)
3 cloves garlic (finely chopped)
1 tsp thyme (chopped)
3 large carrots (finely chopped)
2 star anise
400ml vegetable *nage*

Pork Tenderloin

1 large pork tenderloin (seasoned)
1 tbsp vegetable oil, 2 cloves garlic
1 sprig rosemary, butter (knob of)

To Serve

kale (steamed)

terrine mould (lined with greaseproof paper)

Method

For The Confit Pork Belly (Prepare ahead)
Blend the garlic, oil and salt together. Rub into the pork belly, cling film and refrigerate for 24 hours.
Preheat the oven to 160°C (fan).
Wash the belly under cold water, then pat dry. Place into a deep oven tray, pour in the duck fat and cover with tin foil. Roast for 6-7 hours, cool to room temperature. Transfer the belly to sit in between 2 trays, put a 5kg weight onto the top tray and refrigerate until cold. Cut into 4.

For The Cider Glazed Pork Cheek And Jowl (Prepare ahead)
Preheat the oven to 160°C (fan).
Colour the vegetables and add to a deep oven tray with the cheeks. Pour in the cider, add the peppercorns and herbs, cover with tin foil and cook for 10 hours. Cool to room temperature. Separate the jowl from the cheeks; the jowl is the flat layer of white meat, the cheek the ball of dark meat. Pass the remaining liquid into a pan, discarding the vegetables. Reduce to roughly 200ml, skimming any fat from the surface, to a syrupy glaze.

For The Hog's And Black Pudding Terrine (Prepare ahead)
Preheat the oven to 200°C (fan).
Bring the butter to the boil with the garlic, herbs and truffle oil and leave to cool. Thinly slice the potatoes on a mandolin and add immediately to the butter.
Assemble the terrine by layering 2 layers of potatoes between each layer of the puddings. Once assembled, cover with tin foil. Bake for 1 hour until the potatoes have softened. Press overnight in the fridge with a little weight on it. Cut into 2½cm slices.

For The Salt Baked Heritage Carrots
Preheat the oven to 200°C (fan).
Combine the dry ingredients, slowly adding the water to form a dough. Knead for 1 minute.
Roll to ½cm thick on a floured surface. Carefully wrap around each carrot, covering completely. Bake on an oven tray for 50 minutes, leave to cool. Discard the dough. Cut the carrots in half.

For The Carrot And Star Anise Purée
Sweat the shallot, garlic and thyme until translucent. Add the carrots, star anise and *nage*. Simmer until the carrots are cooked, remove the star anise. Blend and pass through a fine sieve. Season to taste.

To Serve
Sear the tenderloin in the oil in a large frying pan over a medium heat until golden brown. Reduce the heat, then add the garlic, rosemary and butter. Baste for 2 minutes, rest for 5 minutes.
Slowly crisp the pork belly skin in a little oil over a medium heat. Turn over, add a little butter and gently heat through. Heat the cheek and jowl in the cider glaze. Crisp the terrine slices in a hot pan. Drizzle the carrots in olive oil and warm under a low grill. Serve as pictured.

BITTER CHOCOLATE MOUSSE, BEETROOT SALT CARAMEL MOUSSE, PISTACHIO PARFAIT

SERVES 6

 *Els Pyreneus Maury Rouge
(France)*

Ingredients

Bitter Chocolate Mousse
150g bitter dark chocolate
20g unsalted butter
40g good quality cocoa powder
100g caster sugar
50ml water
2 large eggs, 1 egg yolk
200ml double cream

Tempered Chocolate Cylinder
100g dark chocolate
10g white cocoa butter powder

Beetroot Salt Caramel Mousse
225ml full-fat milk
175ml double cream
1 vanilla pod (scraped)
3 egg yolks
80g caster sugar
15g plain flour, 15g cornflour
100g salt caramel
100g roasted beetroot purée

Chocolate Crumb
50g unsalted butter (slightly softened)
50g caster sugar
50g ground almonds
50g plain flour

Pistachio Parfait
3 large eggs
125g caster sugar
2 tbsp water
1 vanilla pod (seeds of)
250ml double cream (semi-whipped)
100g roasted, *blanched* pistachios (blitzed to
a powder)

6 x 20cm acetate strips
6 x 5cm diameter plastic rings

Method

For The Bitter Chocolate Mousse
Melt the chocolate, butter and cocoa powder together over a *bain-marie*. Whisk the whole eggs and egg yolk to soft peaks, then heat the sugar and water in a small saucepan to 115°C. Whisk the syrup into the egg mix, whisking until cool. Carefully fold half of the egg mix into the chocolate, then add half the cream, the remaining egg mix, and finally the remaining cream. Set in the fridge for 4 hours.

For The Tempered Chocolate Cylinder
Melt the chocolate in a *bain-marie*, stirring constantly, to 55°C. Cool to 28°C, then heat again to 32°C. Carefully sieve in the cocoa powder, stirring until dissolved.

Paint the chocolate on the acetate strip with a small pastry brush. Carefully roll into a ring with the chocolate facing the inside of the cylinder. Place inside the plastic ring and leave on a tray to set. Once set, remove from the ring very carefully and peel off the acetate.

For The Beetroot Salt Caramel Mousse
Heat 175ml of the milk, the cream, vanilla seeds and pod on a low heat.

Whisk the egg yolks, sugar, flour and cornflour together. When the milk starts to steam, add to the egg mix, whisking continuously. Return the pan to a low heat and stir until thick. Pass through a fine sieve and combine with the salt caramel and beetroot purée. Cool a little before adding the remaining milk.

If in possession of a creamer gun - this will make a lighter mousse - load the mix to the fill level, screw the top on and charge with just 1 canister. Alternatively, leave to set in the fridge for 12 hours.

For The Chocolate Crumb
Preheat the oven to 170°C (fan).

Combine all the ingredients and spread onto a baking sheet. Bake for 16 minutes, stirring well halfway through. Leave to cool. Break up by pulsing in a blender.

For The Pistachio Parfait (Prepare ahead)
Whisk the eggs to a soft peak. Boil the sugar and water to 120°C, then carefully add to the eggs with the vanilla, whisking until cold. Carefully fold in the cream, then the pistachio powder. Set in the freezer.

To Serve
Quarter fill the chocolate cylinder on the serving plate with the crumb. Fill up to three quarters with the chocolate mousse and top with the beetroot mousse. Finish with a scoop of parfait.

THE WHITE HART

Main Road, Fyfield, Abingdon, Oxon, OX13 5LW

01865 390 585
www.whitehart-fyfield.com Twitter: @the_whitehart

I n 2005 Mark and Kay Chandler took over this historic 15th Century chantry and have lovingly restored it to its former glory. Original features abound, including a secret tunnel to Fyfield Manor, built as an escape route during the time of the dissolution of the monasteries. Housing one of the most stunning interiors of any dining establishment, customers can choose to eat under the soaring eaves of the great hall, up high in the minstrel's gallery or in the cosy bar by the fire.

A firm believer in using local seasonal produce, Mark catches his own crayfish, forages in local woodlands and has developed a large kitchen garden. Local farms and suppliers are supported and menus often feature villagers' surplus produce, including trout caught at the local reservoir. Cooking is modern British with its slow roasted pork belly, with foot long crackling, being a favourite amongst the well-heeled members of the Oxfordshire and Cotswolds society.

Customers are at the heart of this business and service is first class. Mark and Kay have a great team who share their passion and dedication for bringing outstanding food and an unforgettable experience to every customer who walks through the door.

Accolades are plentiful and richly deserved. As well as entries in the Good Food and Michelin Guides, The White Hart has held 2 AA Rosettes for culinary excellence for eight years and, more recently, was crowned Best Gastropub and Restaurant of the Year at the Oxfordshire Restaurant Awards 2015.

The restaurant opens up to a spectacular Medieval arch-braced roof, a perfect setting for chef Mark's wonderful creations - blending depth of flavours from his kitchen garden with his eye for rich colours and striking presentation.

GARLIC CUSTARD WITH WILD MUSHROOM TOASTIE

SERVES 4

Picpoul de Pinet, Domaine de la Madonne 2014
(France)

Ingredients

Garlic Custard

2 heads garlic
olive oil (drizzle of)
225ml double cream
100g egg yolk
sea salt
black pepper

Wild Mushroom Toastie

4 banana shallots (finely diced)
1 tbsp olive oil
500g mixed wild mushrooms (finely chopped)
1 sprig thyme leaves (picked, chopped)
10 wild garlic leaves (finely shredded)
truffle oil (drizzle of)
8 slices medium sliced white bread
50g butter

Garnish

pea shoots (handful of)

4 ramekins

Method

For The Garlic Custard

Preheat the oven to 180°C (fan).

Cut the tops off the garlic heads and drizzle with olive oil. Roast for approximately 30 minutes until soft. Squeeze the roasted garlic cloves out of their skins into a small saucepan.

Add the cream, egg yolk, salt and pepper to the pan. Warm over a medium heat until the custard reaches 85°C.

Pass the custard through a sieve into a jug. Pour immediately into 4 ramekins. Cool to room temperature.

For The Wild Mushroom Toastie

Gently sauté the shallots in a little olive oil over a medium heat until soft but not coloured. Add the mushrooms and thyme to the pan. Increase the heat to high and cook until the mix is dry.

Stir in the wild garlic leaves and season to taste. Add a few drops of truffle oil. Spread the mix generously onto 4 slices of bread and place the remaining slices on top to make 4 sandwiches. Remove the crusts.

Heat the butter in a large frying pan and place the toasties in. Cook until golden brown, turn over and repeat. Remove from the pan and cut into 3 rectangles.

Chef's Tip

If wild garlic is not in season, then use 2 fresh chopped garlic cloves instead.

To Assemble The Dish

Warm the custards under a hot grill until slightly browned on top. Serve with the toasties. Garnish with fresh pea shoots.

MONKFISH WELLINGTON & BROWN SHRIMP GRAVY

SERVES 4

 Pinot Noir, The Edge, Martinborough 2014
(New Zealand)

Ingredients

Monkfish Wellington

500g monkfish fillet (trimmed, portioned into
4 x125g pieces)
sea salt
20 large spinach leaves (steamed, refreshed, dried)
500g pack ready-rolled puff pastry (cut into
4 rectangles)
1 egg yolk (beaten)

Prawn Mousse

½kg whole tiger prawns (raw, peeled and
de-veined, heads and shells reserved)
sea salt (pinch of), 1 large egg
250-300ml double cream
100g peeled brown shrimp
1 tbsp dill (chopped)

Pancakes

1 large egg
400-450ml full-fat milk
200g plain flour, 1 tbsp dill (chopped)
1 tsp vegetable oil (plus more for frying)

Brown Shrimp Gravy

mirepoix (1 onion, 2 carrots, 2 celery sticks,
1 small leek) (chopped)
prawn shells (reserved from the mousse)
2 medium-hot red chillies
1 lemon (pared zest of)
1 head garlic (halved)
1 tsp vegetable oil
2 tbsp tomato purée, ½ bottle red wine
500ml brown chicken or veal stock
100g peeled brown shrimp
1 bunch tarragon (chopped)

To Serve

seasonal greens
heritage carrots
baby onions

Method

To Prepare The Monkfish

Sprinkle salt all over the monkfish, wrap in cling film and refrigerate for 1 hour. Thoroughly wash the salt off and pat dry.

For The Prawn Mousse

Place the prawns in a food processor, add a pinch of salt and blend to a smooth purée. Add the egg and, with the machine running, slowly start to add the cream. Pass through a fine sieve. Add the brown shrimps and dill. Refrigerate until required.

Chef's Tip

For the prawn mousse, ensure everything is cold, from the ingredients to the mixer bowl.

For The Pancakes

Beat the egg with 400ml of the milk and whisk into the flour. Add the dill and 1 teaspoon of vegetable oil. The batter should be a similar consistency to single cream. Loosen with the remaining milk if necessary. Allow to rest for 30 minutes. Cook 4 pancakes in a 24cm non-stick frying pan with a little oil.

To Assemble The Wellington

Spread a 1cm thick layer of the mousse, the same width as the monkfish, on a pancake. Place a layer of spinach leaves on top, followed by the monkfish. Roll the pancake to completely cover the monkfish and fold in the ends. Roll this in a rectangle of puff pastry, brushing the joins with beaten egg yolk to seal. Wash the whole pastry with egg. Repeat with all the monkfish pieces. Refrigerate for at least 30 minutes.

For The Brown Shrimp Gravy

Sweat the *mirepoix*, prawn shells, chillies, lemon rind and garlic in a little vegetable oil until softened but not browned. Add the tomato purée and cook for 1-2 minutes. Pour in the wine and boil until well reduced and syrupy. Add the stock and reduce until the sauce reaches the desired consistency. Pass through a fine sieve and reserve.

To Serve

Preheat the oven to 190°C (fan).

Cook the Wellingtons for 20 minutes.

Warm the gravy through and, at the last minute, add the brown shrimp and tarragon.

Cut the ends off the Wellingtons and slice in half.

Drizzle the brown shrimp gravy around the plate and serve with seasonal greens, heritage carrots and baby onions.

PISTACHIO SPONGE WITH CHERRIES

SERVES 6

 Sauternes, Carmes de Rieussec 2009 (France)

Ingredients

Drunken Cherries

100ml brandy
25g caster sugar, 25ml water
200g ripe sweet cherries

Cherry Purée

1kg sweet ripe cherries (stoned, stalks removed)
200g caster sugar, 100ml water
2 lemons (juice of)

Cherry Jelly

200ml cherry purée
2½ leaves gelatine (soaked in cold water)

Cherry Sorbet

200ml cherry purée
100ml water
55g caster sugar, 20g glucose
½ lemon (juice of)

Cherry Meringue

3 egg whites
200g caster sugar
50ml cherry purée

Pistachio Cake

3 eggs, 180g caster sugar
150ml milk, 300g plain flour
160g ground pistachios
1½ tsp baking powder

Vanilla Mascarpone

50g icing sugar
200g mascarpone
1 vanilla pod (seeds of)

Garnish

6 mint leaves
50g ground pistachios
20g toasted pistachios

20cm square cake tin (lined with parchment)

Method

For The Drunken Cherries (Prepare ahead)

Bring the brandy, sugar and water to a simmer. Remove from the heat. Once cool, pour over the cherries. Place in an air-tight jar and refrigerate. Marinate for at least 5 days.

Chef's Tip

Leave the drunken cherries to marinate for as long as possible to intensify flavour. They can be kept up to 4 months in the fridge.

For The Cherry Purée

Add all of the ingredients to a saucepan and simmer for 30 minutes until the cherries are soft. Blitz in a food processor and pass through a sieve.

For The Cherry Jelly (Prepare ahead)

Bring the purée up to the boil. Stir in the gelatine. Pass through a sieve and pour into a container lined with cling film. Refrigerate overnight. When set, portion into 1cm cubes.

For The Cherry Sorbet

Place all the ingredients in a saucepan and bring to the boil. Remove from the heat and allow to cool completely. Churn in an ice cream machine and freeze.

For The Cherry Meringue

Preheat the oven to 100°C (fan).

Whisk the egg whites on full speed, until frothy. Add the sugar 1 spoonful at a time (keep whisking). Once the mix becomes stiff, slowly add the cherry purée. Spread the mix on a baking tray lined with baking parchment. Bake for 45 minutes or until crispy but not coloured.

For The Pistachio Cake

Preheat the oven to 180°C (fan).

Beat the eggs and sugar together until pale, light and fluffy. Slowly add the milk. Fold in the dry ingredients until just combined. Pour into the tin and bake for 50 minutes.

For The Vanilla Mascarpone

Sieve the icing sugar into the mascarpone. Add the vanilla seeds, mix and refrigerate.

To Assemble The Dish

Cut the pistachio cake into strips and trim off the crust. Place on a plate, swipe the cherry purée and then artfully arrange the other elements.

186
WILD GARLIC
RESTAURANT & ROOMS

3 Cossack Square, Nailsworth, Gloucestershire, GL6 0DB

01453 832 615
www.wild-garlic.co.uk Twitter: @TheWildGarlic

This family run restaurant is now a Cotswold foodie destination thanks to chef patron Matthew Beardshall's playful and inventive cooking. Matthew's strong pedigree was earned working with kitchen heavyweights such as Gordon Ramsay, Marcus Wareing, Martin Blunos and Darren Velvick.

Matthew is serious about the produce that comes into his kitchen; quality and sustainability are always in mind, meaning menus are reassuringly short and dishes showcase the wonderful, seasonal produce from the surrounding Five Valleys. Keep an eye out for surprise elements to dishes, Matthew likes to keep diners guessing.

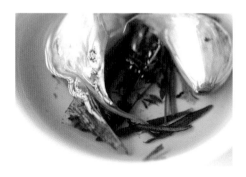

The stylish dining room is refreshingly contemporary and the service is professional yet warm and sincere. Regular diners love the six-course tasting menu complemented with beautifully matched wines. Wild Garlic is a great place for a relaxed lunch with friends or a celebratory dinner.

For a more laid back experience, try the restaurant's wine and tapas bar, serving a selection of classic and contemporary tapas dishes and cocktails. For an invigorating start to your day, try the brunch menu served Friday - Sunday from 10am. The Sun Terrace at Wild Garlic is the perfect spot to read a paper and enjoy the sunshine.

Complete your stay in this lovely undiscovered part of the Cotswolds in one of the three beautiful airy rooms: two of which have large bay windows overlooking picturesque Cossack Square.

Matthew's cooking collates together a perfect selection of innovative dishes to provide an incredible experience with a strong focus on flavour, alongside elements of playfulness.

WILD GARLIC, LABNEH & DUKKAH WITH SMOKED AUBERGINE & PARMESAN

SERVES 4

 Mád, Dry Furmint, Tokaji, Mád, 2014 (Hungary)

Ingredients

Labneh
200ml natural organic yoghurt

Smoked Aubergine
1 aubergine
2 cloves garlic (finely chopped)
olive oil (drizzle of)
salt (to season)

Parmesan Crisp
100g Parmesan (finely grated)

Dukkah
50g sesame seeds
20g coriander seeds
40g hazelnuts
20g ground cumin
1 orange (zest of)

To Serve
4 wild garlic leaves

Method

For The Labneh (Prepare ahead)

Put the yoghurt into a clean tea towel and tie it up in the fridge to drain, with a bowl underneath to catch the whey. Hang for at least 3 hours or overnight depending on what texture you prefer.

For The Smoked Aubergine

Cook the aubergine directly on the stove top flame and turn as each side chars. Leave to cool, then cut in half and carefully scrape all of the flesh out. Gently fry the garlic in a little oil, then add the aubergine and cook for 2-3 minutes. Season with salt, then purée in a food processor.

For The Parmesan Crisp

Preheat the oven to 180°C (fan).

Arrange the Parmesan in small discs on a baking tray lined with parchment paper. Bake for 6-8 minutes.

For The Dukkah

Toast off all the seeds and nuts then blitz in a food processor for 1 minute. Add the zest and a pinch of salt.

To Assemble The Dish

Roll a spoonful of the labneh in the dukkah, then roll in a wild garlic leaf. Add dots of the aubergine purée and some pieces of the Parmesan crisp.

Chef's Tip

Wild garlic is perfect for a beginner forager; found in abundance from March-May in wooded areas around the country. Don't confuse it with Lily of the Valley, the easiest test is to crush a leaf in your hands and you will get a strong garlic, spring onion smell. Get permission and pick off the beaten path. Out of season you can use vine leaves instead.

RUMP OF COTSWOLD LAMB, MARINATED AUBERGINE & PERSILLADE

SERVES 4

 Calmel & Joseph, Terrasses du Larzac, Languedoc 2013 (France)

Ingredients

Marinated Aubergine

15g ginger (roughly chopped)
3 cloves garlic (roughly chopped)
1 red chilli (roughly chopped, optional)
3 vine tomatoes (roughly chopped)
60g honey
60ml red wine vinegar
1 sprig rosemary
1 fresh bay leaf
1 sprig thyme
1 aubergine
40g extra virgin rapeseed oil (for frying)

Persillade

½ bunch curly parsley
½ bunch wild garlic leaf
½ lemon (zest of)
1 shallot (finely diced)
2 cloves garlic (finely chopped)

Lamb

4 x 250g lamb rumps
oil (for frying)

To Serve (optional)

seasonal vegetables (purple sprouting broccoli, cavolo nero, kale, green beans)

Method

For The Marinated Aubergine (Prepare ahead)

Place the ginger, garlic, chilli, tomatoes, honey, vinegar and herbs in a pan and bring to the boil, then pour into a deep, metal dish.

Cut the aubergine into wedges and colour the cut sides in a smoking hot pan with a good splash of oil. Transfer the charred aubergine into the warm marinade. Leave to cool and refrigerate overnight in a sealed container. This is best marinated overnight but can be used straight away.

Chef's Tip

Make lots of the aubergine, it's great as an antipasti.

For The Persillade

Chop the parsley and wild garlic roughly, taking care not to bruise it (a sharp knife is a must). Simply mix all the ingredients together. It will keep for a few days in the fridge, but is best made fresh. Try mixing any leftovers with oil and use it instead of a pesto.

For The Lamb Rump

Preheat the oven to 200°C (fan).

Seal the lamb rump in a hot pan with a touch of oil and colour all sides until golden brown. Transfer to the oven for 8 minutes, then leave to rest for 8 minutes.

To Assemble The Dish

Roll the lamb rump in some of the persillade, then slice into 3. Gently warm the aubergine in the marinade over a low heat. Arrange on the plate as pictured. Finish with a spoonful of persillade and garnish with the chopped chilli, garlic and tomato from the marinade. Serve with seasonal vegetables.

CHESTNUT & CHOCOLATE MOUSSE

SERVES 4

🍷 *Edmond Briottet, Crème de Châtaigne Liqueur,*
Dijon (France)

Ingredients

Chestnut Sponge

120g sugar
4 large eggs (separated)
200g thick natural yoghurt
1 lemon (zest of)
125g chestnut flour
salt (pinch of)
1½ tsp baking powder

Chestnut And Chocolate Mousse

100g 70% dark chocolate
75ml double cream
50ml full-fat milk
½ large egg (beaten)
125g sweetened chestnut purée

Crystallised Chocolate

100g sugar
20ml water
100g dark chocolate

Garnish

caramelised chestnuts (diced)
rum and raisin ice cream (optional)

4 rings (lined with cling film), ramekins or
dome moulds
30cm x 45cm baking tray (lined with
parchment paper)

Method

For The Chestnut Sponge

Preheat the oven to 180°C (fan).

Whisk the egg yolks and sugar until thick and creamy. Stir in the yoghurt and lemon zest.

Sift the flour, salt and baking powder and fold in carefully.

Whisk the egg whites in a clean bowl until they form stiff peaks. Fold into the batter very gently. Pour into the baking tray and bake for 12-16 minutes, turning halfway. Leave to cool, then cut out discs to make the base of your dessert. Place into your desired mould. This makes more sponge than required but it freezes well and works really well in a tiramisu.

Chef's Tip

The chestnut sponge makes this a great gluten-free alternative. Make sure that the baking powder you use is gluten-free too.

For The Chocolate Chestnut Mousse (Prepare ahead)

Blitz the chocolate in a food processor for 30 seconds.

Bring the cream and milk to the boil and pour onto the chocolate. Blitz for 1 minute. With the motor still running, add the egg and blitz for another minute. Add the chestnut purée and blend for a further 1 or 2 minutes until smooth. Pour on top of the sponge in the dishes. Leave the mousse to set for 6 hours in the fridge, overnight is better. If you are working ahead, you can freeze the mousse at this point. Remove from the freezer 1 hour before you want to serve them.

For The Crystallised Chocolate

Bring the sugar and water to the boil in a pan. Keep heating until the temperature reaches 150°C. If you don't have a sugar thermometer, keep boiling until it just starts to caramelise around the edge. Remove from the heat and add the chocolate immediately. Mix with a fork until it resembles a chocolate crumble.

To Assemble The Dish

Turn the mousse onto the serving plates. Garnish with the crystallised chocolate and caramelised chestnuts. In the restaurant we serve it with a rum and raisin ice cream.

FISH

FLYING FISH SEAFOODS
Unit 9 & 10, Indian Queens Workshops, Indian Queens,
Cornwall, TR9 6JP.
T: 01726 862 876 www.flyingfishseafoods.co.uk
*Flying Fish Seafoods is proud to supply high quality fish to
distinctive restaurants and hotels throughout the South and
West of England. They source the finest, freshest fish directly
from Cornwall's best fishermen directly to your door.*

KINGFISHER BRIXHAM
Torbay Business Park, Unit 4/5 Woodview Road,
Paignton, TQ4 7HP.
T: 01803 553 232 www.kingfisherbrixham.co.uk
*Kingfisher Brixham is set in a prime coastal location.
They source, supply, prepare and deliver quality fresh fish
and seafood to the catering industry in the South West.*

SIMPLY FISH
Unit 6, Buller Quay, East Looe, Cornwall, PL13 1DX.
T: 01503 262 442 www.simply-fish.co.uk
*Suppliers of local fresh fish straight from the boats at
Looe Harbour.*

STEVENSONS OF NEWLYN
Newlyn, Penzance, Cornwall, TR18 5HB.
T: 01736 362 998 www.newlynfreshfish.co.uk
*Suppliers of fresh fish sourced from Cornish waters -
deliveries twice daily.*

VENTNOR HAVEN BAY FISHERIES ON THE ISLAND
Eastern Esplanade, Ventnor, Isle of Wight, PO38 1JR.
T: 01983 852 176
*Ventnor is renowned for its quality crab and lobster but
Geoff and his team serve up a whole selection of daily
catches which varies with the seasons and is prepared in
the fishery seven days a week. If you're looking for the
Island's freshest locally caught fish and shellfish, Ventnor
Haven Fishery is a must!*

WING OF ST MAWES

Unit 4, Warren Road, Indian Queens Industrial Estate, Indian Queens, Cornwall, TR9 6TL..

T: 01726 861 666 www.wingofstmawes.co.uk

Robert Clifford-Wing founded Wing of St Mawes in the fishing village of St Mawes, Cornwall over 25 years ago and is still heavily involved with the day-to-day running of the business. Now located at a bigger premises in Indian Queens, Wing of St Mawes buy fresh fish, shellfish and seafood daily from the fish markets of Newlyn, Plymouth, Looe and Brixham in Cornwall and Devon.

MEAT

KITTOWS BUTCHERS

Kilhallon Farm, Kilhallon, PAR, PL24 2RL.

T: 01726 814 926 www.kittowsbutchers.co.uk

Makers of award-winning sausages and hogs pudding. Producers and purveyors of finest Cornish quality meats. They run their own small herd of Pedigree Red Ruby beef cattle and now their own Kilhallon herd of Pedigree Dexter cattle on the original farm from where their great great grandad started it all in the late 1800s. Hog roast machines are also available for hire.

POOLE BATTEN RARE BREED PORK FARM

Burrington, Umberleigh, North Devon, EX37 9NG.

T: 01769 581 852 www.poolebatten.co.uk

Poole Batten pork comes from animals born, raised and allowed to mature at a natural pace, on grass, without hurrying the process or by feeding artificial growth promoters. Breeders of rare breed traditional British pigs and purveyors of the highest quality pork to fine butchers, high-end restaurants, delicatessens and the more discerning consumer.

FINE FOOD, ARTISAN & SPECIALITY FOODS

FOREST PRODUCE

Colliton Barton, Broadhembury, Honiton, Devon, EX14 3LJ.

T: 01404 841 847 www.forestproduce.com

Suppliers of fresh vegetables, cheeses, cured meat and fish and dry goods.

198 LARDER

TOTAL PRODUCE UK
2-5 Callywith Industrial Estate, Launceston Road, Bodmin, Cornwall, PL31 2RQ.
T: 01208 77911 www.totalproduce.com
Total Produce has become one of the UK's largest and most accomplished fresh produce providers, with an extensive network of depot operations throughout the UK, reaching from Cornwall to Edinburgh. Providing all produce needs from plough to plate.

FRUIT & VEGETABLES

LIVING LARDER
Galley Horne, Apse Heath, Isle of Wight, PO36 0JT.
T: 01983 717 164 www.livinglarder.co.uk
A family-based supplier on the Isle of Wight that grows 70% of their own fruit and the vegetables. Customers who order a veg box will also receive a weekly recipe card with tried and tested family favourites.

WESTCOUNTRY FRUIT SALES
The Distribution Centre, Higher Argal, Budock, Falmouth, Cornwall, TR11 5PE.
T: 01326 372 304 www.apassionforfood.co.uk
One of the oldest fresh produce wholesalers in Cornwall. A family run business with roots going back as far as 1856.

DAIRY

BEN LAY'S FREE RANGE LTD
Manor Farm, Fyfield, Abingdon, Oxfordshire, OX13 5LR.
Farmer Ben has supplied free range eggs to The White Hart at Fyfield for 10 years. He also supplies Waitrose.

VALE HOUSE KITCHEN

The country skills and cookery school

Loves Hill, Timsbury, Bath, Somerset, BA2 0EU
T: 01761 470 401 www.valehousekitchen.co.uk

Vale House Kitchen is a bespoke country skills and cookery school in the village of Timsbury, eight miles outside Bath. We offer a range of cookery and baking courses, and a unique opportunity to acquire or hone fishing, shooting, foraging and butchery skills. Courses cater to all levels and are taught by the very best of the South West's culinary professionals. Eight to ten participants per class ensures an intimate, hands-on and inspiring experience.

Why choose Vale House Kitchen?

- Enhance your passion for food by learning how to find, catch, shoot, prepare, cook and present it.
- Award-winning professional tutors teach small classes, and focus on practical, one-to-one direction.
- State-of-the-art kitchen workstations and demonstration area, fully equipped by Smeg.
- Our beautiful rural setting has easy access to Bath, Bristol and beyond.
- Cook with the finest locally sourced ingredients.
- Learn about and love local food as much as we do.

WHITE PEPPER
COOKERY SCHOOL

White Pepper is one of the most impressive cookery schools in the South West, annually recognised by national awards, including The British Cookery School Awards and The UK Cookery School Awards.

Nestled in the heart of rural Dorset, yet only a stone's throw away from Poole Harbour and the Jurassic coast, the cookery school attracts students from across the UK. Time Out London recently called the setting 'gorgeous'.

White Pepper attracts beginner and intermediate cooks as well as aspiring professionals. Its recreational courses include cookery breaks, weekend, one day, short and 'quick cook' sessions.

With the backing of the Confederation of Tourism and Hospitality, White Pepper's Chef School delivers an internationally recognised qualification.

In fact, this cookery school has most bases covered, offering a Kids' Cookery School, bespoke cookery for private groups and White Pepper Corporate.

The spacious kitchen premises stand in a converted barn at Bere Farm, providing an exceptional environment in which to learn new culinary skills. The school works hard to maintain a dynamic style of teaching through its various expert tutors, who are all qualified and experienced professionals.

White Pepper's signature courses include Beside the Sea, Bread at Bere Farm, Feathered and Furred, Forage Fungi and French Patisserie.

For further information please visit www.white-pepper.co.uk or call 01202 280 050

AL DENTE

Al dente describes vegetables that are cooked to the 'tender crisp' phase - still offering resistance to the bite, but cooked through. Al dente can also describe cooked pasta which is firm but not hard.

BAIN-MARIE

A pan or other container of hot water with a bowl placed on top of it. This allows the steam from the water to heat the bowl so ingredients can be gently heated or melted.

BLANCH

Boiling an ingredient before removing it and plunging it in ice cold water in order to stop the cooking process.

CARTOUCHE

A piece of greaseproof paper that covers the surface of a stew, soup, stock or sauce to reduce evaporation.

CHINOIS

A conical sieve with an extremely fine mesh. It is used to strain custards, purées, soups and sauces, producing a very smooth texture.

CLARIFIED BUTTER/CLARIFYING

Milk fat rendered from butter to separate the milk solids and water from the butter fat.

CONFIT

A method of cooking where the meat is cooked and submerged in a liquid to add flavour. Often this liquid is rendered fat. Confit can also apply to fruits - fruit confits are cooked and preserved in sugar, the result is like candied fruits.

EMULSION/EMULSIFY

In the culinary arts, an emulsion is a mixture of two liquids that would ordinarily not mix together, like oil and vinegar.

FRENCH TRIMMED

To French trim, fat, meat or skin is cut away to expose a piece of bone, so that it sticks out.
It also means that any excess fat is cut off. French Trimming can be done to lamb chops and bigger cuts;
it can even can be done to chicken legs or breasts.

GASTRIQUE

A caramelised sugar, deglazed with vinegar, used as a flavouring for sauces.

JULIENNE

A culinary knife cut in which the vegetable is sliced into long thin strips, similar to matchsticks.

MIREPOIX

Finely diced combination of celery (pascal, celery or celeriac), onions and carrots. There are many regional mirepoix variations, which can sometimes be just one of these ingredients, or include additional spices creating a rich, flavoursome base to sauces or stews.

NAGE

A term for a flavoured liquid used for poaching delicate foods, typically seafood. A traditional nage is a broth flavoured with white wine, vegetables and herbs, in which seafood is poached. The liquid is then reduced and thickened with cream and/or butter.

PANE

To coat with flour, beaten egg and breadcrumbs for deep frying.

QUENELLE

A neat, three-sided oval (resembling a mini rugby ball) that is formed by gently smoothing the mixture between two dessert spoons.

SABAYON

Made by beating egg yolks with a liquid over simmering water until thickened and increased in volume. The liquid can be water, but Champagne or wine is often used.

SOUS VIDE

French for 'under vacuum.' A method of cooking food sealed in airtight plastic bags in a water bath or in a temperature-controlled steam environment for longer than normal cooking times. The intention is to cook the item evenly, ensuring that the inside is properly cooked without overcooking the outside, and to retain moisture.

201
HINTS & TIPS...

HOW TO MAKE ICE CREAM WITHOUT A MACHINE

Although relatively inexpensive these days, not everyone has access to an ice cream machine. That's no reason not to follow some of these delicious recipes found in the Relish South West book. Although more time consuming than a machine, excellent results can be obtained by following this simple method.

Follow the recipe right up until it tells you to churn in the machine, including any chilling time in the fridge.

Take your mixture from the fridge and stir with a rubber spatula. Transfer it to a suitable plastic container with a lid. There should be at least 2cm space at the top to allow the mixture to expand when freezing. Cover and place in the freezer for two hours.

Remove from the freezer and beat with a hand mixer, still in the container, to break up the ice crystals that are beginning to form. Cover and return to the freezer for a further 2 hours. (If you don't have a hand mixer then you may use a fork and some 'elbow grease' to break up the crystals).

Remove from the freezer and beat again with the hand mixer. The ice cream should be thickening up nicely at this point but too soft to scoop. Return it to the freezer for an additional hour. Beat again. If your ice cream is still not thickened sufficiently, repeat this process again after another hour. When the ice cream has thickened properly, stir in any add-ins at this point (honeycomb, nuts...). Do not beat with the hand mixer after the add-ins have been mixed in.

Place the tightly sealed container in the freezer and allow the ice cream to freeze until firm. The ice cream should be removed from the freezer 15-20 minutes before you wish to eat it. This will make scooping easier.

This method will also work for sorbets. Sometimes sorbets may go a bit 'icy' or 'crumbly' if left for too long in the freezer. This can be rectified by blitzing in a food processor just before serving.

Duck Egg Custard Tart, Apple Puree, Cinnamon Ice Cream - **Page 084**

HOW TO MAKE A SUGAR STOCK SYRUP

This makes about 750ml sugar stock. It can be stored in a sterilised jar in the fridge for a couple of months.

500g white sugar
500ml water

Place the sugar and water in a pan. Dissolve slowly over a very low heat. You must not allow the syrup to boil until all the sugar has dissolved, about 5 minutes. Once completely dissolved, bring to the boil, then simmer for 5 minutes.

CALLING ALL CHEFS! ISN'T IT ABOUT TIME YOU FEATURED IN ONE OF OUR BOOKS?

Relish Publications is an independent publishing house based in North East England. The business was founded on an award-winning series of restaurant guides and recipe books featuring each region across England, Scotland and Wales. Relish has now worked with over 1,500 leading chefs and restaurants, building a portfolio of beautifully illustrated guides which are stocked nationally in Waterstones, Harvey Nichols, in each featured restaurant, in leading independent stores and online globally.

Relish has a small, friendly professional team, with experience in publishing, print management, editing, proofing, photography, design and artwork, sales distribution and marketing.

Relish Publications ensure a personal approach to every single customer, working exceptionally hard to develop a great product which reflects each chef's talent and passion.

Duncan and Teresa Peters established the company in 2009, with a vision of building a niche publishing house for food lovers. The success of Relish is now reflected in the fact that they have an ongoing programme of regional books, with many regions now having a Second and Third Helping (edition) of the leading restaurant guide and dozens of independent commissions from internationally celebrated chefs including Jean Christophe Novelli and Mark Greenaway.

To find out how your chef or restaurant can be featured or discuss your publishing requirements simply log on to our publishing website www.relish-publishing.co.uk or call our head office on 01670 571 635 and speak to one of our team.

HERE'S WHAT SOME OF BRITAIN'S BEST CHEFS HAVE SAID ABOUT WORKING WITH RELISH

"Relish books are full of enjoyable recipes and ideas for making the most edible treasures we have on our doorstep; both places to eat them and new, exciting ways to cook them."
Angela Hartnett, MBE

"The Relish cookbook offers the home cook some great inspiration to make the most of these wonderful ingredients in season." *Tom Kitchin, The Kitchin, Edinburgh*

"With mouth-watering, easy to follow recipes and beautiful photography, this book is a must have for any foodie, from professional chef to the inspired home cook."
Michael Caines MBE

Relish Midlands is a fantastic recipe book that brings together so many of the talented chefs and quality restaurants in the area. It gives you a taste of what our exciting region has to offer as well as the encouragement to try some new recipes. *Adam Stokes*

"Relish Wales Second Helping has been lovingly created and showcases the very best of our beautiful land. Great chefs, great food and sumptuous dishes. It makes for essential reading and I'm proud to be part of it." *James Sommerin*

"The Relish team has truly been amazing to work with. To have produced my book within two months from start to finish, only shows how professional a team of people can be."
Jean-Christophe Novelli

CONVERSION CHART

COOKING TEMPERATURES

Degrees Celsius	Fahrenheit	Gas Mark
140	275	1
150	300	2
160-170	325	3
180	350	4
190	375	5
200-210	400	6
220	425	7
230	450	8
240	475	9

*Temperatures for fan-assisted ovens are, as a general rule, normally about 20°C lower than regular oven temperature.

WEIGHT MEASUREMENT CONVERSIONS

1 teaspoon (5ml/5g)	$1/4$ oz
1 tablespoon (15ml/15g)	$3/4$ oz
10g	$1/2$ oz
25g	1oz
50g	2oz
75g	3oz
150g	5oz
200g	7oz
250g	9oz
350g	12oz
450g	1lb

VOLUME MEASUREMENT CONVERSIONS

55ml	2 fl oz
150ml	$1/4$ pt
275ml	$1/2$ pint
570ml	1 pt
1 litre	$1^{3}/4$ pt